Bicycle Day and other Psychedelic Essays

Alan Piper

Published by
Psychedelic Press
London, UK

ISBN: 9781916266766

We would like to express our eternal gratitude to the anonymous artist who created the
Bicycle Day cyclist that we have adapted for this cover. The first of many trips.

Copyediting: Nikki Wyrd
Design and typesetting: Peter Sjostedt-Hughes

For more information:
www.psychedelicpress.co.uk

Contents

Acknowledgements

The collected essays in this book would never have been published without the support and encouragement of several people. I must thank Carl Ruck and Mark Hoffman of *Entheos* journal and Guillaume Gris of *Invisible College* journal for early encouragement, and necessarily the staff at Psychedelic Press especially for publishing work of mine that sometimes challenges comfortable assumptions concerning the history of psychedelic culture. Regarding my Bicycle Day essay, Sandra Lang who is currently engaged in post-doctoral research on science and society at University of Zurich provided helpful comments and suggestions. So did Karl Baier, Professorial Research Fellow at the University of Vienna, who agreed to include what amounts to a transcription of his lecture 'Early Psychonauts: Albert Hofmann's Occultic Network'. Other associates in the cultural history of psychedelics offered both direct and indirect encouragement. I must make a special mention for Andy Roberts and Mike Jay. In line with other home-based authors, I must also thank my long-suffering wife June.

Foreword

— Mike Jay —

When does the history of psychedelics begin? In the consensus that underpins our current psychedelic 'renaissance', their original era began in the 1950s, when mescaline and LSD first hit the headlines as vision-inducing compounds and were hailed by psychiatrists as a possible cure for schizophrenia. This answer is uncontroversial, indeed tautologous, in the narrow sense that the word 'psychedelic' was only coined in 1956: it is vain to search for it prior to that date. But it doesn't follow that western science, philosophy, literature and culture had never considered mind-expanding drugs—with all their profound implications for medicine, the mind, society and reality itself—until that point. The obvious follow-up question, rarely asked, is how much of the original psychedelic era was entirely new, a creation of that mid-20th-century moment—and how much was the rediscovery, or rebadging, of a deeper history?

Advocates typically project their claims for psychedelics onto a chemically transfigured future rather than delving into their contested history. Most are content to look no further back than the oft-told origin stories: Albert Hofmann's bicycle ride in 1943, Aldous Huxley's first mescaline trip in the Hollywood Hills in 1954. Those who claim a longer history for psychedelic culture usually locate it in the misty past of prehistoric or pre-Christian Europe, or find parallels in the traditional practices of non-western societies in distant corners of the globe. It's rarely considered that the psychedelic era embraced by the 1960s counterculture might itself have been a renaissance: the rediscovery of a far more recent story, much closer to home, that had been relegated to the margins of western thought during the drug-averse early decades of the 20th century.

Alan Piper has been exploring these 20th-century margins with quiet persistence over many years, excavating the foundations of the psychedelic era and exposing its roots among the thinkers and writers of the previous generation. Drawing on previously neglected modernist sources, German literature in particular, he presents us with peyote circles at Harvard in the 1920s, mystical drug initiations in interwar fantasy and feminist fiction, and curious premonitions of LSD in Weimar Germany.

In the title piece of this collection, Piper takes Albert Hofmann's seminal 'bicycle day' self-experiment with LSD and exposes the network of forgotten precursors and influences that informed it, from the ergot researches of Hofmann's employer, Arthur Stoll, to the prodigious imaginations of Stoll's friend Hermann Hesse and Hofmann's intellectual mentor, Ernst Jünger. In the process, he uncovers a literary milieu and wisdom school that profoundly influenced the generation to come as they considered how novel reality-transforming drugs might be seeded and nurtured in the disenchanted landscape of 20th-century modernity. His path through the labyrinth of untold stories behind the legendary episode leads us into the buried strata of chemistry, botany, poetry, philosophy and spirituality from which psychedelics would eventually emerge.

1

The Legacy of Transgression

Psychedelics and the End of History

L SD and other psychedelic substances currently occupy a curious position. While their proponents once revelled in their transgressive status, they now wish for these drugs 'to come in from the cold' and return from a period of isolation, concealment and exile to circles of deserved esteem. Ironically, for drugs that were once the touchstone of alterity, when being hip meant 'have you been turned on?', their advocates now seek the legitimacy of medical and scientific authority, along with a legally recognised sacramental status.

I presented a paper at the Breaking Convention conference in 2015 with this situation in mind.[1] Against the background of a burgeoning 'Psychedelic Renaissance', I asked the audience if the medicalisation of psychedelics, necessarily provided by Big Pharma and regulated by medical authorities, and the approval of psychedelics for spiritual purposes in limited legally recognised circumstances, will mean they 'lose their mojo?'[2] Meaning, will they lose the radically enlightening quality often ascribed them, in which psychedelics de-programme the user from the meta-narratives of Church, State and consumer society that condition us to accept the status quo?

This question has continued to preoccupy me as an aspect of my ponderings on the territory of psychedelics and their associated counterculture ever since. I've been greatly assisted in this consideration by my discovery of Isernhagen's *Acid against Established Realities*[3] and Leung's *Ecstasy and Transcendence in the Postmodern State*.[4] Isernhagen, for instance, supports a belief I had already reached, which was that when psychedelics emerged in the mid-20th century they were co-opted by a pre-existing culture of resistance to modernity. He writes:

> One might begin by asking why drugs acquired such cultural significance in the 1960s and 1970s at all. In my view this was because there already existed a well-established cultural tradition - that of aesthetic modernism (ca. 1900/1910 -?) which was searching for what one might term alternate realities: there also existed a well-established language to express this search and its results.[5]

Both Isernhagen and Leung focus on the transgressive nature of psychedelics. Isernhagen takes a negative view of psychedelic culture. He sees it as part of a perpetual subculture; an 'underbelly' that struggles against the surplus repression demanded by everyday life. A subculture in which 'there is only the attempt, after the transgression of boundaries, or the recognition that they have become permeable, to keep them fluid, uncertain and shifting, but all the same real'.[6] In other words, a permanent state of liminality, an endless immersion without intent or conclusion.

On the other hand, Leung argues for the legitimisation of the religious aspects of psychedelic experience and does this partly by reference to the transgressive nature of psychedelic experience as a route to the sacred. For Leung the psychedelic experience promotes transcendent perspectives and values which transgress the dominant ideology of consumer capitalism that places the highest value on rationality, logic, efficiency and productivity. She references Taussig's essay on transgression, which argues that by an inverted logic in modernity, sacrilege becomes the place where the sacred is most likely to be experienced;[7] one might say a left-hand path.

As early as 1948, with LSD still hardly known even in the scientific community,[8] the prominent German author and drug adventurer Ernst Jünger wrote to Albert Hofmann about the latter's own reports to him on LSD, suggesting to Hofmann that this was perilous territory. 'It seems indeed that you have entered a field that contains so many tempting mysteries' he wrote. 'These are experiments in which one sooner or later embarks on truly dangerous paths and may be considered lucky to escape with only a black eye.'[9] Later, in 1961, Hofmann expressed his own concern to Jünger about the possible transgressive nature of psychedelics:

> I must admit that the fundamental question very much occupies me, whether the use of these types of drugs, namely of substances that so deeply affect our minds, could not indeed represent a forbidden transgression of limits.[10]

It is striking that the two friends should be discussing the LSD experience in transgressive terms well before the counterculture and associated moral panics of the 1960s and '70s concerning psychedelics. However, the modern sense of the words 'drug' and 'literature' date to the Romantic period of Keats, Coleridge and de Quincey. Indeed, it is in the late 18th and early 19th century in which a literature of intoxication and addiction first emerged, investing both with the glamour of the transgressive and forbidden.[11] What though is transgression or transgressive behaviour?

Transgression can be defined as the violation of a law, a duty or moral principle, or otherwise the action of going beyond or overstepping some boundary or limit. In terms of society, it means socially disruptive acts, breaking local laws, customs or taboos. In terms of the natural order of being, it means the abnormal, the artificial or deviant and in terms of the sacred order of being it includes the blasphemous or sacrilegious. A transgressive action can be one of neglect or omission, but when deliberately employed by a counterculture it often assumes the deliberate intention to shock or offend.

The decadents and aesthetes of the *fin de siècle* wanted to shock the comfortable middle classes out of their self-righteous complacency, to '*épater la bourgeoisie*'. It was a battle cry that resonated from Baudelaire's *Fleurs du Mal* (1857) to the Italian artist Piero Manzoni's *merda d'artista* (1961), an artwork consisting of his own tinned shit, and well beyond. Acts of transgression tend to be those that damage or violate the integrity of a structure. In terms of people it includes acts that expose oneself or others to shocking or dangerous experiences with the possibility of physical or psychological harm. For the body it can mean acts such as self-mutilation, tattooing or scarification, or for the mind methods of disrupting normal mental processes through fasting, self-isolation or, crucially here, the use of psychoactive drugs.

The concern expressed by Hofmann in 1961, given the then legal status of LSD, lay not merely in the profound alteration of the senses, but significantly in overstepping a boundary, something of the character of accessing arcane knowledge or experiences. There is a familiar aspect of psychedelic experience that is hard to pin down but is, regardless of initial confidence, a 'what on earth have I done to myself?' conviction, as a drug kicks in. It is a sense that you have entered a dangerous zone of forbidden experience, from which you may not return as the same person or perhaps not at all.

The psychedelic culture of the 1960s and '70s was intimately associated with counter-cultural political radicalism, opposition to the war in Vietnam, as well as exciting developments in the arts, which psychedelics are considered to have catalysed. Social histories of psychedelic culture tend to focus on psychedelics' role in fuelling a revolt against the post-war conservative culture of the

1950s.[12] However, long before the psychedelic Sixties there existed a counterculture that rejected the same aspects of 20th century Western culture that characterised the countercultural revolutionaries of the 1960s. That opposition, termed modernism, was a reaction against the characteristics of modernity in Western industrialised nations. Namely, against enlightenment rationalism (considered as essential for the provision of social and scientific progress) and to the materialism of consumer culture (as supported by capitalism, industrialisation and mass production). It also opposed the strictures of institutionalised religion and the enmity of nation states, which were expressed through acts of conscientious objection to serving in the two World Wars.

This pre-existing counterculture often promoted natural living, vegetarianism and utopian communalism. From the turn of the century, arcadian communities were established such as the artists' colony of Monte Verità in Ascona, Switzerland, which championed modernism in the visual arts, dance and theatre, together with health reform and nude sunbathing.[13] A return to traditional skills and handicrafts was promoted by the Arts and Crafts movement led by William Morris. In terms of spirituality and religion people turned to heterodox gnosis, the Greek mysteries, spiritualism and occultism through groups such as The Theosophical Society, The Society for Psychical Research and magical orders such as the Hermetic Order of the Golden Dawn.

Largely expressed through the media of art, literature, music and film, this counter-movement has come to be termed modernism and its exponents modernists, who somewhat confusingly opposed modernity. Abandoning traditional notions of harmony, music explored the dissonant, starting with the Clause Debussy (1862–1918) and on to the free jazz of Ornette Coleman (1930–2015), until the ear eventually became accustomed to what had previously seemed discordant or cacophonous. In the visual arts there was the development of the fragmentary techniques of collage, composed of clippings from newspapers and street advertisements, reflecting the overwhelming impact of expanding methods of mass communication. Random assemblage of texts and images might reveal hidden meanings, as in the cut-up techniques later popularised by William Burroughs. Art was made from discarded everyday items as *objets trouvés*,[14] such Picasso's 'Bull's Head' made from a bicycle seat and set of rusty bicycle handlebars, which has a parallel in the psychedelic experience which stimulates the perception of meaningful images in random objects.

Philosopher Williams James coined the term 'stream of consciousness' in *The Principles of Psychology* (1890). It was later applied to a new style of writing that reflected naturalistic, free associative, streams of thought and images, with James Joyce's modernist novel *Ulysses* (1922) being a famous example. For the modernists, novel mind states and transgression were the points where individuals could find personal gnosis versus religious orthodoxy and received wisdom, and an authentic existence versus social conformity. Illumination in this counterculture was sometimes sought by a deliberate derangement or bypassing of rational processes. Thus, the famous quote from Rimbaud:

> The poet makes himself a seer by a long, prodigious, and rational disordering of all the senses... For he arrives at the unknown... and even if, crazed, he ends up by losing the understanding of his visions at least he has seen them![15]

Interestingly, this counterculture had an ambiguous relationship with science and technology. While some turned to what others may have deemed the irrational, scientific developments also emphasised the importance of unseen forces and immaterial realms through reference to the powers of electricity, magnetism, X-rays and quantum physics. One might also include evolutionary theory, Marxism and psychoanalysis. All of which were theories that depicted surface appearances as the product of unseen forces, whose meaning, patterns and mode of operation could only be revealed and understood by specialists and explained using technical language. Science was engaged in service of the search for proof of unseen forces that would explain phenomena such as psychokinesis and telepathy. One might recall Aleister Crowley's famous remark: 'Our method is science, our aim is religion'. There is a certain irony that those committed to a belief in occult powers or the paranormal turned to science to prove their case, but science was in turn interested in testing the claims of the occultists and parapsychologists, in case they had unearthed phenomena of interest or possible service,[16] an uneasy relationship that persists into the present day.[17]

The burgeoning science of psychiatry sought to categorise and qualify the status of various altered states, including those characterised as mental illness. Between 1919 and 1921 the art historian and psychiatrist Hans Prinzhorn was employed by the University of Heidelberg to collect art made by people institutionalised due their mental health. It was published in 1922 as *Bildnerei der Geisteskranken* (Artistry of the Mentally Ill)[18] and was associated with the studies of mescaline at the University conducted by Kurt Beringer (1893–1949), in which Prinzhorn himself participated.[19] There was a crossover between the interest of psychiatry in the art of the mentally ill and the interest in such art by the avant-garde. Salvador Dalí and Paul Klee found inspiration in the Prinzhorn collection, [20] while the Nazis felt that avant-garde art duplicated such works or was of the same degenerate character, and seized and exhibited it as such.[21]

According to Isernhagen the psychedelic Sixties 'dominant mode and mood were the same transgression of boundaries that characterizes the 20th century's other avant-gardist innovations.'[22] In connection with William James' late 19th century investigations into the effects of psychoactive drugs, he notes 'the coincidental emergence of the modernist concern with alternate realities and the scientific exploration of those outskirts of the mind where religious and drug-induced experiences take place.'[23] In early accounts of the experience of psychoactive drugs, such as that by Havelock Ellis, who succeeded in obtaining a supply of peyote buttons in England in 1897,[24] the boundaries between personal literary accounts and medical experimentation were yet to be clearly defined. [25] Drugs such as mescaline from the 1920s onwards and LSD from the 1950s were the ideal drugs of the modernist aesthetic of intellectual and spiritual experimentation and exploration. They were disruptive of normal perceptions and forms of understanding, but also provided novel forms of awareness and insight, and for processes of deep self-examination. They provided an awareness of inner, normally unconscious processes and a sense of awareness of external universal processes, unifying man and cosmos.

All these readings contribute to the reasons why there was an enthusiastic adoption of psychedelics as a key technology for transgressing normal limits of perception and experience by a pre-existing subculture resistant to a status quo that placed a high value on rationality, social order and the productive processes of capitalist enterprise. However, when the LSD inspired baby boomers of the Sixties proclaimed, 'we are the people our parents warned us about', as the children of a generation perked up on amphetamines and sedated with barbiturates, they may well have been primed for an all-American 'better living through chemistry'.[26] Regardless, the children of the 1960s and '70s took up their transgressive legacy and ran with it in a heady mixture of LSD, radical politics and sexual freedom, a revolution that made Timothy Leary in President Richard Nixon's eyes 'the most dangerous man in America'. Chris Jenks argues that transgression 'has become the modern, post-God initiative, a searching for limits to break, an eroticism that goes beyond the limits of sexuality. God becomes the overcoming of God.'[27] In a similar vein, Michael Taussig writes,

> intoxication as an explosively dislocating and reconfiguring mystical force... is a dangerous territory, but one we cannot avoid in discussing transgression and modernity at the end of the twentieth century, with drugs as much if not more than sex occupying a strategic position in politics, revolution, counterrevolution and the sacred.[28]

These statements reflect the tenet of modernism as a movement that believed enlightenment was to be found in the extremes of human experience, including the deliberate derangement of the senses and the outcome of random processes.

The use of psychedelic drugs thus found a natural home in the environment of the modernist aesthetics of the avant-garde, providing for a positive interpretation of anomalous experiences under the influence of psychedelics, which could be and were also interpreted as typical of a disordered mind when classed as 'psychotomimetics'.[29] In this way psychedelics became a 'technology of resistance' in service of the pre-existing oppositional consciousness of modernism, and within countercultural circles of the Sixties became the touchstone of alterity.

According to the latter-day psychedelic pundit Terence McKenna:

> Psychedelics are illegal not because a loving government is concerned that you may jump out of a third story window. Psychedelics are illegal because they dissolve opinion structures and culturally laid down models of behaviour and information processing. They open you up to the possibility that everything you know is wrong.[30]

This is an attractive idea and one that chimes with the notion that psychedelics fuelled the revolutionary 1960s. There is truth in what McKenna claimed because without doubt psychedelics became a tool of resistance to the status quo and an icon of the counterculture, but does it overlook what makes psychedelics fundamentally transgressive in social terms?

Unfortunately, the inability of governments to distinguish between the different character of psychedelics and drugs such as heroin, amphetamines and cocaine impacts on their legal status. Nonetheless, psychedelics do violate fundamental social values because the profound alteration of the senses they induce may be a danger to self or a danger to others, as is the irresponsible supplying of psychoactive drugs to those not suitably prepared for the experience. It should be further observed that historically and transculturally the use of mind-altering drugs has been taboo and subject to ritual restrictions, such as the secrecy on pain of death regarding the Kykeon, the secret psychoactive potion of Eleusinian Mysteries,[31] and the dietary and other restrictions in the traditional use of Ayahuasca and Peyote. In most cultures, strict rules have determined who can and cannot use these powerful substances and when, where and for what purpose.

If psychedelics had remained of interest only to an intellectual elite, as exemplified by Aldous Huxley, Ernst Jünger and Albert Hofmann, their status may well be different today. However, as agents with profound and sometimes confusing and disorientating psychological effects it appears unlikely that they would have indefinitely escaped becoming controlled substances. Even enthusiasts do not consider psychedelic experiences to be without any danger and harm reduction is regularly on the agenda at psychedelic conferences and resourced at music festivals. Timothy Leary wrote in 1963: 'Licensing will be necessary. You must be trained to operate. You must demonstrate your proficiency to handle consciousness-expanding drugs without danger to yourself or the public.'[32] For Terence McKenna the transgressive nature of psychedelics was their threat to the status quo due to their capacity to cut through our social and intellectual conditioning, but his thinking took an eschatological turn.

There is something about the visionary nature of the psychedelic experience that lends itself to a conviction that we are living in the end times or on the verge of enormous change. In McKenna's own words 'the psilocybin-induced cognitive hallucination made the impossible and unlikely seem probable and reasonable.'[33] The sense that Western culture was on a trajectory which would lead to its collapse was famously propounded by Oswald Spengler in *Decline of the West* (1918). In it he wrote, 'it would appear, then, that Western consciousness feels itself urged to predicate a sort of finality inherent in its own appearance.' Similarly, in *The Archaic Revival* (1991), Terence McKenna wrote, 'History is going to end. This is the astonishing conclusion I draw from the psychedelic experience.'[34] It is not difficult to deduce from the psychedelic experience a sense that the culture of the West has exhausted itself.

An end to history here means that the culture of the West has reached its inevitable teleological conclusion, an end implicit in its beginning.

Significantly, McKenna borrowed the idea of an 'Omega Point' from the Jesuit priest Teilhard de Chardin in which the universe returns back to the *logos* from which it originally emerged, and focussed on the year 2012, associated with the Mayan Calendar.[35] He envisaged his end of history as a 'transcendental departure from business as usual'[36] with psychedelics being the agency of immanentising a psychedelic eschaton, in which historical time was characterised by increasing novelty and experienced as an exponential acceleration of biological and technological change.[37]

McKenna's 'end of history', as with Spengler and de Chardin, referred initially to an end of our current cultural epoch and the initiation of a new cultural order, but ultimately took on a cosmological aspect. However, an 'end to history' could mean either the initiation of a new cultural epoch or that human society has reached its final state of cultural development and consciousness, a steady state. Such an alternative conception of an 'end of history' has been proposed by Francis Fukuyama. He envisages it as the global triumph of capitalism, liberal humanism and democracy, with an end to competing ideologies and an infinite and peaceful extension of Western culture.[38]

While awaiting the arrival of McKenna's transition to a new order of being, what place is there for psychedelics in the increasing dominance of Fukuyama's utopian vision of the comforts of consumer capitalism? As we contemplate the possibility of a fully psychedelicised society achieved through a Psychedelic Renaissance, Fukuyama's future consumer paradise, or perhaps a combination of the two, we may need to reassess our fascination with transgression and its power as an agent of transformation and finally perhaps as an end in itself.[39]

In the arts and modern media of the 20th and 21st centuries, acts of transgression occupied such a major role that transgressive acts in the arts have almost become normalised. Artist Carolee Schneemann, in her performance work *Interior Scroll* (1975), undressed, wrapped herself in a sheet and climbed on the table.

> After telling the audience she would read from her book, *Cezanne, She Was a Great Painter*, she dropped the sheet, retaining an apron, and applied strokes of dark paint on her face and body. Holding the book in one hand, she then read from it while adopting a series of life model "action poses". She then removed the apron and slowly drew a narrow scroll of paper from her vagina, reading aloud from it.[40]

Two black and white photographs of Schneemann on the table during the second part of the performance when she was withdrawing the scroll, with a column of text on either side of the photographs which elaborate the words written on the scroll, are now held in the collection of the Tate Gallery in London.[41] Thus what was shocking and transgressive becomes, if not normalised, at least sanctified and enshrined by an august institution as an object of cultural merit. Historian of modernism Peter Gay notes how avant-garde masterworks of the 20th century were 'absorbed into the very cannon their authors professed to despise and had worked to discredit. With time, offensive (or at least startling innovations) … lost their power to outrage'[42] and 'the absorptive capacity of a cultural establishment that modernists had worked so hard to subvert was nothing less than impressive.'[43]

Gay is hardly the only author to have observed the capacity of capitalist culture to absorb, commoditise, sell back and thus neutralise the power of transgressive agents. Bell Hooks, writing about the way in which interactions between racial identities and capitalism can perpetuate systems of oppression, makes a universally important point concerning the transgressive power of something as simple as the symbolic role of styles of dress as icons of difference—one might cite those of Hip Hop or Punk. Their power as agencies and signs of resistance to ignite a critical consciousness is diffused once they are commodified and communities of resistance are replaced by communities of consumption.[44]

In the 1960s and '70s transgressive classics by authors such as the Marquis de Sade and pornography such as the BDSM novel of female submission *The Story of O*,[45] which were once the preserve of private collections, appeared as mass-market paperback copies. Transgression has ultimately moved from niche into the mainstream with the normalisation of hard pornography through the agency of the Internet and with what has come to be termed 'torture porn' in the shape of films such as *Hostel*.[46] Mark Dery, in his essay 'Been There, Pierced That',[47] asks whether we have become un-shockable, and transgression has now been commoditised and sold back to us not only as art, but as entertainment. Is transgression now 'so last century' and has it lost its socially and personally transformative power?

The circulation of extreme material facilitated by photography, film and most recently by the internet has certainly moved the goal posts in terms of what is transgressive. For example, filmic depictions of death in warfare have moved from the essentially bloodless of the 1950s to the shockingly graphic by the end of the century, such as in the otherwise essentially family-friendly *Saving Private Ryan* (1998). Though our capacity to tolerate extremes of expression may have been extended, many universal norms are hard to displace. Though what functions as transgressive is subject to local custom, law, and practice, certain inherently human values remain unchanged, such as what is inside the human body should stay there and not be ripped out in a display of shit and gore. Borders may change according to cycles of conservatism and liberality, but transgression as a technique for radically questioning current values will always be a tactic of the artist, comedian, and seeker of notoriety. The determination to shock with a strategic purpose or merely to achieve celebrity is hardly likely to disappear. Whilst the transgressive power of psychedelics cannot be purged due to their capacity to radically disrupt normal perceptive processes and present endlessly novel ones, it is profoundly muted when employed therapeutically or shaped by dogma.

It was in this scenario that, in my 2015 presentation, I asked the question: 'Have psychedelics lost their subversive mojo and been absorbed into an existing "spiritual supermarket" catering to the cure of bourgeois neuroses and into a developing medical and scientific orthodoxy exploring the therapeutic potential of psychedelics?' I proposed three main overlapping domains of contemporary psychedelic culture. First, the medical and scientific appropriation of psychedelics, in which psychedelics acquire medical and scientific meaning, but operate only within legal and professional restrictions. Second, what might be termed 'sacramental psychedelia', in which psychedelics are styled as having religious meaning, but operate only within cultic doctrinal restrictions. Lastly, I referred to 'recreational psychedelia' which, in defiance of any legal or other restrictions, belongs to the sphere of personal consumption, the experience of which is often best expressed best through music, art and literature. I suggested that only in the realm of recreational psychedelia, outside of the law and sanctioning authorities of State, medical or spiritual authority, do psychedelics retain the power to subvert, challenge and transform our fixed ideas. This was the aspect of the psychedelic experience that was so central to the enthusiasms of Timothy Leary and Terence McKenna, and which is sometimes considered the very purpose of art itself.

Terence McKenna's end of history was hardly going to materialise dramatically in 2012 as part of what became a New Age fascination with the Mayan Calendar but does reflect the tendency of psychedelics to invoke a cosmological view of human culture. That prophetic aspect of McKenna's thinking has dwindled to the image of a street corner merchant of imminent apocalypse. Terence's hope for a future 'transcendental departure from business as usual' has settled into the hope of our current Psychedelic Renaissance for the embrace of psychedelics as a cure for current ills, amongst other things bolstering an urgent need for a universal ecological consciousness. The question is will this take the form of the psychedelicising of culture or the acculturation of psychedelics? For me it is significantly the second and conforms to Fukuyama's vision rather than McKenna's. The psychedelicising of culture has already happened, starting in the 1960s, and really that party is over with psychedelics being embraced by and influential in every aspect of culture, from advertising to music to film, art and literature—to the extent that now if a review of a novel or a film is described like being 'on acid' or is 'acid fried' it is assumed that the reader knows what is meant.

Since I first raised concerns about the medicalisation and commodification of psychedelics in 2015, it has become a hot topic of debate on the internet. Psychedelic pharmaceutical start-ups and those offering guidance on investment in companies developing psychedelics as medicines are advertising widely. Drug tourism, despite its criticism on the grounds of cultural appropriation and its neo-colonial character, remains popular. I would argue that, once commodified as medicines or sacraments and subjected to tight regulation by medical or legal authorities, psychedelics are entirely amenable to the rhythms of capitalist consumer culture. It is hard not to conclude that under the control of medical authorities or within the ritual and doctrinal strictures of place and meaning in religious settings, psychedelics are a caged tiger. One that is harnessed to the everyday requirements of our consumer culture and in those contexts serves only to reproduce everyday life as we know it. However, the unregulated and sometimes chaotic disordering of the senses, in search of otherwise hidden orders of being, will remain the domain of the artist, philosopher and bohemian outsider. There is no doubt that psychedelics fulfil a fundamental human desire for the dramatic but temporary overturning of our usual modes of understanding and perception. This after all is the very nature of the psychedelic experience, which although sometimes discomforting, is an experience that some choose to return to again and again.

The enduring fascination with psychedelics is indicative of a fundamental human appetite for experiences in which the normal constraints of our individual identities and the regulation of our perceptions required for the accomplishment of day-to-day tasks are both revealed to us and fundamentally disrupted. It is a desire that is best enjoyed outside any form of hegemonic control, where that desire can most fully express itself. There is a deep human resistance to any control over the desire to loosen the reins on our consciousness and allow it to display its capacity for a fundamental exuberance.

Notes

1   A full videographic archive of presentations from the Breaking Convention conferences is available at: https://www.youtube.com/c/BreakingConvention

2   The full video of the original presentation 'Psychedelics, Transgression and the End of History' retitled as 'Alan Piper - Psychedelic Drugs: Sacred & Profane' is available at: https://youtu.be/S-HjEtDvve0

3   Isernhagen 1993

4   Leung 2011

5   Isernhagen 1993: 122

6   Ibid. 129

7   Taussig 2006: 171

8   In 1948 just one paper concerning the mental effects of LSD had been published, by Arthur Stoll's son Werner who worked as a psychiatrist at the Burghölzli clinic in Zurich, which Hofmann had shared with Jünger. Stoll, W. A. Lysergsaure-diathyl-amid, ein Phantastikum aus der Mutterkorngruppe. Schweiz.Arch.Neur. 60 (1947). Source: *Bibliography on Psychotomimetics 1943–1966*. Reprinted with permission of Sandoz Pharmaceuticals by US Department of Health, Education & Welfare, Public Health Service. National Institute of Mental Health. RM315.Z9 S23.

9   Letter from Jünger to Hofmann 3/3/1948. Hofmann 1979: 156-7

10 Letter from Hofmann to Jünger, 16 December 1962. Hofmann 2009: 164

11 Boon 2009

12 See for example: Lee & Shlain 1992 and Stevens 1988

13 Green 1986

14 The French for 'found objects' has remained the term used in the world of art.

15 Often cited without a source it is given as 'from a letter to Paul Demeny, May 15, 1871' in Horovitz and Joris: 1995: 43

16 For example, the work of J B Rhine at Duke University in Durham, North Carolina, commencing in the nineteen-twenties.

17 See for example: Ronson 2004

18   'Art of the mentally Ill', Prinzhorn 1922. Prinzhorn's study has remained of permanent interest and been published in multiple languages and an English translation is available (Prinzhorn 1972).

19   Röske 2004

20   English 2022

21   Ibid.

22   Isernhagen: 1993: 122

23   Ibid.: 122

24   Ellis 1902

25   Berridge 1988: 56

26   This phrase was derived from an advertising slogan of the Dupont chemical company and used with intended irony on pin badges and posters celebrating LSD, as it originally promoted the contribution of Dupont's products to the sparkling efficiency and cleanliness of the modern American life.

27   Jenks 2003: 90

28   Taussig 2006: 172

29   'Psychotomimetic' was a classification for drugs that were thought to mimic the symptoms of psychosis and applied to LSD in the 1950s, but largely abandoned as too reductive in favour of 'psychedelic' by the 1960s.

30   https://psychedelicsalon.com/podcast-197-mcnature/

31   Wasson, Ruck, Hofmann 1978

32   Alpert & Leary 1963

33   Jenkins 2014: 87-88

34   McKenna 1992: 18

35   Jenkins 2014: 87-95

36   McKenna 1992: 18

37   Abraham, McKenna, Sheldrake 1992: 159

38   Fukuyama 2012.

39   Jenks 2014: Inside cover review by Martin Jay, University of California, Berkeley.

40   See   https://www.tate.org.uk/art/artworks/schneemann-interior-
      scroll-p13282. I have removed some parenthesised references to
      Schneemann's works from the website article.

41   Ibid.

42   Gay 2008: 9

43   Ibid.: 11

44   Hooks 2015: 33

45   First published in France 1955, the Paris based Olympia Press
      published the first English edition in 1965.

46   *Hostel* (2005) Directed by Eli Roth. Lions Gate Films.

47   Dery 2012: 234-239

2

Jazz Age Peyotism at Harvard

A Psychedelic Circle with a Mormon Connection

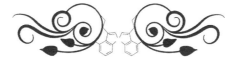

In Don Lattin's *The Harvard Psychedelic Club* (2010), the author tells us how Timothy Leary, Ram Dass, Huston Smith, and Andrew Weil killed the post-war conservative culture of the 1950s and ushered in a New Age for America by proselytising the use of psychedelic drugs. However, they may in fact have been the 'Johnny-come-latelies' of a Harvard psychedelic culture that first took root in the 1920s. Drawing from biographical and autobiographical accounts of experimentation with peyote by students and tutors at Harvard in the late Teens and early Twenties, a picture emerges of considerable recreational use in that milieu. Some of those involved went on to be poets, novelists and radical activists of note.

The story begins with Alan M Wald's *The Revolutionary Imagination* (1983), a study of the relationship between Harvard-educated avant-garde poets in the 1920s and Marxist politics. He documents how poet

Sherry Mangan, a 1925 Harvard graduate with honours in Classics, 'was part of a group that experimented with hallucinogenic drugs.'[1] Most of this group, including S. Foster Damon, John Brooks Wheelwright and Robert Hillyer, were members of a student group termed the Harvard Aesthetes. It was composed largely of aspiring poets who found inspiration in decadent and transgressive ideals of the English aesthetes of the 1890s, such as Oscar Wilde and Aubrey Beardsley, and in the French Decadents such as Baudelaire and Verlaine.[2] The Harvard Aesthetes, a label they themselves eschewed, were described somewhat satirically as composed of 'young men who sat cross-legged in purple pyjamas, sipped exotic liqueurs in rooms heavily hung with brocades and silks, and burned incense before curious bronze figures.'[3]

Wald notes that Virgil Thomson, the famous American composer, mentions in his autobiography that he first learned about peyote at the end of World War One from a minister, and that he introduced the drug to S. Foster Damon and others of the Harvard Aesthetes, who adopted its use with enthusiasm:

> Sherry (Mangan) developed his own system of obtaining mescal caps by mail from New Mexico for the peyote parties in his room in Weld Hall [a Harvard dormitory]. Ground up and taken in a glass of water, the caps were a very bitter brew; after the students had drunk it, they put their heads out the window to be certain it would stay down. At one of these parties the toilet seat in Sherry's bathroom was mysteriously burned and the current wise crack was that someone in his hallucinations must have thought he was a comet.[4]

Mangan, who was to pursue a career that combined being a correspondent for *Time-Life* journals and a radical Trotskyite activist,[5] began his heavy drinking at Harvard which continued during later visits to Cambridge and Boston, where he further experimented with peyote.[6] He expressed his unreserved admiration for Virgil Thomson who 'insisted always on being in complete control of himself and would not dream of going to a length with the drug or with alcohol where he could not instantly act as one completely sober'.[7]

> Virgil Thomson's co-experimenter, S. Foster Damon (1893–1971), born in Newton, Massachusetts, was later to become an American academic, a specialist in William Blake, a critic and a poet. He married Louise Wheelwright, sister of John Wheelwright (another of the Aesthetes). Damon had graduated from Harvard University in 1914, returning there after World War I as an instructor in the English Department.[8] When Thomson described his experiences with peyote to Damon, he was intensely interested and wanted to try it. Damon, Thompson and Robert Hillyer would take peyote together about ten times over the next few years. It clearly had a profound effect on Damon who started reading *The Occult Review*[9] and between 1922–1923, the magazine published six articles by Damon, chiefly on alchemical topics.[10]

Damon intuited the Cabbalistic connections in Blake's writings; both this connection and his peyote experiences are referred to by Allen Ginsberg in his introduction to Timothy Leary's *High Priest* (Leary 1968). Damon's book *William Blake, His Philosophy and Symbols* (1924) was later followed by *A Blake Dictionary* (1965), the work for which he is perhaps best known. Here he refers to Blake's imagery having the characteristics of the effects of peyote visions: 'the thought-emotions which rose from his subconscious inevitably took human form in visual symbols, with a vividness and completeness comparable to the color-visions of peyote.'[11]

Virgil Thomson fondly recalls Foster Damon in his autobiography:

> I do not remember how I first knew him; but I do remember long walks and talks; and I remember him bringing me music and books that he thought I ought to know … (some) changed my life. Among these last were the piano works of Erik Satie, a pile of them four inches high, and a thin small volume called Tender

Buttons, by Gertrude Stein. I returned these favors by introducing him to peyote, which we would take together, sometimes with another poet and English instructor Robert Hillyer.[12]

Robert Hillyer graduated from Harvard in 1917, after which he went to France and volunteered with the Ambulance Corps serving the Allied Forces in World War I. He had long links to Harvard University, including holding a position as a Professor of English. He was a member of the Epsilon chapter of the prestigious St. Anthony Hall Delta Psi fraternity at Trinity College in Hartford, Connecticut. Hillyer is not kindly remembered by some Ezra Pound scholars, who associate him with his 1949 attacks in the *Saturday Review of Literature* on Ezra Pound's 'The Pisan Cantos' due to Pound's overt anti-Semitism, following Pound's controversial award of the 1948 Bollingen Prize in Poetry.

Peyote-using Harvard Aesthetes, like John Wheelwright and others, are connected with the literary circles formed around Gertrude Stein, Mabel Dodge Luhan, and the international Bohemian culture of New York, Florence and Paris. John Wheelwright met the writer and salonnière Mabel Dodge Luhan in one of the centres of Bohemian culture, Florence, where she held court at her Villa Curonia. She later moved to New York's Greenwich Village, where she immersed herself in its radical avant-garde culture.[13] There in 1914 Luhan organised a peyote ceremony at her apartment in Greenwich Village, led by the archaeologist and ethnologist of Pueblo culture Mark Raymond Harrington (1882–1971), who also supplied the peyote. The ceremony started well but fell into chaos when Luhan absented herself; some of the participants became panic struck, while others had profound religious experiences.[14] Luhan later campaigned against the decriminalisation of peyote for members of the Native American Church. This was despite having moved to Taos, New Mexico, due to her sympathy for native American culture, where she wed a Native American husband. The personal, political and tribal politics involved there were complex, not all Native American elders approved the adoption of the peyote rite.[15]

The Harvard Aesthetes included the novelist John Dos Passos, a friend of the Swiss-born poet and writer Blaise Cendrars,[16] who in turn was a friend of Alexandre Rouhier author of *Le Peyotl, la plante qui fait les yeux émerveillés* [Peyote the plant that fills the eyes with wonder] (1927), whom Cendrars referred to as 'L'épopée du peyotl' [the Pope of Peyote].[17] Rouhier was connected with the Parisian occult *demi-monde* of the 1920s[18] and was a supplier of peyote in Europe at that time, which he cultivated in the south of France. The Polish artist, photographer, playwright and drug adventurer Stanisław Ignacy Witkiewicz, who painted portraits under the influence of various drugs, recording which particular drug or drugs by cyphers written in the corner of the paintings, refers to Rouhier as a source of peyote.[19]

The student member of Harvard Aesthetes, responsible for introducing them to peyote, was the aforementioned Virgil Thomson, the American composer who later wrote an operatic score for Gertrude Stein's *Four Saints in Three Acts* (1927/28). He was born in Kansas City, Missouri and as a child he befriended Alice Smith, granddaughter of Joseph Smith, founder of the Church of Latter-day Saints. In his autobiography, Thomson records Frederick Madison Smith, third Prophet-President of the Reorganized Church of Jesus Christ of Latter Day Saints,[20] 'passing the previous winter, for his wife's health, in the Southwest, [where] he had made inquiries about a hallucinogenic cactus known as peyote, as a student of man's higher powers, notably those of second sight and prophecy.'[21]

It was Frederick Smith, head of an offshoot of the Latter-day Saints denomination, who was the 'minister' that introduced Thomson to peyote. Smith was none other than the grandson of Joseph Smith (1805–1844), founder and prophet of the Church of the Latter-day Saints, better known as the Mormon church.[22] The Church forbade drugs, but Frederick Smith did not believe that peyote was, technically, a drug. To him it was 'a natural substance, an ancient means to tap one's inner powers derived from a hallucinogenic cactus.' Smith had read

Havelock Ellis about powers of peyote and in Texas he had observed Native American Indians who ate the plant and Catholic converts 'who made from it a tea for communion.'[23]

Dr Smith was a believer in the powers of prophecy and vision, and his grandfather's accounts of his own visions were the foundation of the Mormon religion. Frederick Smith's PhD dissertation, later published as *The Higher Powers of Man* (1918), was a study of ecstatic states and devoted a whole chapter to a sympathetic study of the peyote religion. One night Dr Smith described to Virgil his own experiences with peyote and their coloured visions, and Virgil asked if he might try it. Dr Smith obliged, and Thomson went to bed with a supply of buttons, the effects of which lasted the entire night:

> Full visions each as complete in color and texture as a stage set, began slowly to appear before my closed or open eyes, then came more rapidly till two hours later they were flashing at least twice every second, with no delay involved in their complete perception. Each one, moreover, had a meaning, could have been published with a title, and their assembled symbolisms or subjects, though not always sequentially related, constituted a view of life not only picturesque and vast, but just as clearly all mine and all true.[24]

By Smith's own account he had participated in the peyote rite himself and went through this ceremony several times as recorded in the *Saints Herald*, an official periodical of the Church of Latter-day Saints.[25] According to an account by Shelby M Barnes in another Latter-day Saints journal;

> believing that the peyote experience first released then enhanced the human mind toward creative expansion, he understandably encouraged others to use the drug. One such example concerned Virgil Thomson. Thomson, who was to become a famous composer and long-time music critic at the *New York Times,* a college friend of Smith's oldest daughter, Alice.[26]

Interestingly, the possible use of psychoactive plant drugs by Joseph Smith, the founder and prophet of The Church of Jesus Christ of Latter-day Saints, is explored by Dr Robert Beckstead in his paper 'The Restoration and the Sacred Mushroom: Did Joseph Smith Use Psychedelics to Facilitate his Visionary Experiences?' presented at the Sunstone Symposium (2007).[27]

The Harvard Aesthetes' willingness to explore the psychoactive properties of peyote reflects their identification with the late Victorian Aesthetes' taste for the exotic, and the French decadents' penchant for the mind-altering effects of opium, hashish, and absinthe. Virgil Thomson's introduction to peyote by Frederick Smith might appear to be the product of a chance encounter, but it was on the basis of Smith's conviction that a man of the arts would provide him with a worthwhile 'itemized report' of the effects of peyote that he offered it to Thomson.[28] The fledgling modernist poets of the Harvard Aesthetes' experimentation with peyote reflects the early 20th-century avant-garde's persistent interest in the connection between creativity and non-ordinary states of mind.

The circulation and availability of peyote, whether in dried form or as Anhalonium (an extract), and its influence amongst the avant-garde of the interwar period may be greater than is generally accepted. Descriptions tend to be confined to brief accounts in biographies or autobiographies, as in the case of Virgil Thomson. The English author Mary Butts, a close friend of Thomson, wrote frankly about her drug experiences in her journals (2009) and, as Soror Rhodon, is credited by Aleister Crowley for her assistance drafting his *Magick Book 4* while she was staying at Crowley's colony at Cefalù in the early 1920s.[29] While Crowley may have personally used peyote with serious Magickal intent, James Laver,[30] a contemporary who was well positioned to comment on the follies and excesses of the 'bright young things' of the era, reports how Aleister Crowley freely dispensed peyote at parties and that; 'Crowley's disciples used to take Anhalonium, the effect of which was to enlarge the consciousness and give "a different dimension". Even those who weren't exactly disciples were sometimes given packets of the drug.'[31]

All these associations paint a picture of experimentation with peyote in the 1920s that encompassed recreational use, psychological experimentation, and an interest in its traditional role in Native American religions; one that prefigures the popular psychedelic culture engendered by the members of Don Lattin's *Harvard Psychedelic Club.*

Notes

1   Wald 1983: 77

2   Freedman 1993: 122–123

3   Carr 2004: 57

4   Ibid.

5   See: https://www.trotskyana.net/Trotskyists/Bio-Bibliographies/ bio-bibl_mangan.pdf

6   Wald 1983: 82

7   Ibid.

8   It would appear that S Foster Damon, like Robert Hillyer, was a tutor at the time of his involvement with peyote at Harvard.

9   Tommasini 1997

10   These editions of the journal can be sourced through http:// iapsop.com, a US-based private organization focused on the digital preservation of Spiritualist and occult periodicals.

11   Damon 2013: 436

12   Thomson 1966: 46

13   Luhan 1993 : passim

14   Luhan 1985: Ch. XI, 'Peyote'

15   Stewart 1987: Ch. 8

16   Carr 2004: 269–274

17   Cendrars 2006 : 196

18   Rivière 2009 : 75–76

19   Gerould & Witkiewicz 1992: 209

20   A breakaway denomination of the Latter Day Saints movement.

21   Thomson 1966: 42

22   Though commonly referred to as the Mormon Church and its members as Mormons, this Christian denomination is properly referred to as The Church of Jesus Christ of Latter-day Saints and some church members may dislike the use of the term Mormon. However, for the sake of brevity and the familiarity of the term for readers I have used it here.

23   Tommasini 1997: 83

24   Thomson 1966: 42

25   'A Trip Among the Omaha Indians' in *Saints Herald:* Nov. 26, 1919. 1151–1154

26   Barnes 1995: 91-97

27   A recording of the presentation is available at https://sunstone. org/the-restoration-and-the-sacred-mushroom-did-joseph- smith-use-psychedelics-to-facilitate-his-visionary-experiences/ A transcript can be found at http://www.mormonthink.com/files/ restoration-sacred-mushroom.pdf

28   Thomson 1966: 43

29   Crowley 1989: 922

30   James Laver (1899–1975) is best known as a historian of fashion and art on which he published widely, but he also had an interest in the occult and published well-researched works on Nostradamus (1942) and J K Huysmans (1954). Through this connection he visited Crowley during his last days at Netherwood. See Clayton 2012.

31   Laver 1963: 118

3

Drugs, Sapphism and Altered States in Hope Mirrlees' *Lud-in-the-Mist*

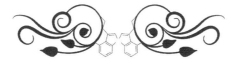

Hope Mirrlees' fantasy novel *Lud-in-the-Mist* (1926) was largely forgotten and out of print until 1970. It was then republished as part of the Ballantine paperback Adult Fantasy series, during a boom in popular fantasy and science fiction literature that owed something to the influence of psychedelic drugs.[1] Hope Mirrlees thus joined the ranks of other rediscovered authors of 19th- and early 20th-century fantasy works, such as Lord Dunsany, William Morris and ER Eddison, who were also published in the series. However, despite having earned an entry in encyclopaedias of fantasy and science fiction, Mirrlees and her novel remained essentially obscure. It was not until a recent wave of interest in early 20th century female modernist writers, and the development of critical work on fantasy genres, that there has been a general re-evaluation of her talents and place in literary history.

How can one describe Hope Mirrlees' novel *Lud-in-the-Mist*? Part fairy tale, for it definitely concerns fairies; part ghost story, as there is at least one ghost, who plays an active part in the story; part crime novel, for there is a crime whose perpetrators are unmasked and punished; and it is assuredly a drug novel, for the story revolves around the effects of a 'mysterious drug'.[2] The core narrative concerns the pernicious influence of 'fairy fruit' on the youth of a bourgeois merchant class in the fantasy realm of Dorimare. Celebrated contemporary fantasy author Neil Gaiman describes *Lud-in-the-Mist* as the 'single most beautiful, solid, unearthly, and unjustifiably forgotten novel of the 20th century ... a little golden miracle of a book.'[3] He goes further, describing it as 'a mystery tale and a Mystery tale,'[4] suggesting that there is something recondite to be found in its pages, perhaps even something initiatory.

Lud-in-the Mist was conceived and written while the author lived in Paris in the 1920s. It was then 'a city whose very name could be shorthand for sapphism,'[5] writes Mary Beard, 'the city of Gertrude Stein, Natalie Barney, Una Troubridge, Alice B. Toklas[6] — and later, we shall wonder, of Jane Harrison and Hope Mirrlees.'[7] Mirrlees and her life partner, the Cambridge classicist Jane Ellen Harrison, moved there immediately after Harrison's retirement from Cambridge in 1922. That Mirrlees and Harrison's relationship was a sapphic love relationship, was the understanding of their friend and an occasional publisher of their works, Virginia Woolf, who described their apartment in Paris as a 'Sapphic flat' in a letter to Mary McCarthy.[8]

Being conceived and written during Mirrlees and Harrison's sojourn in 'Paris Lesbos' might in itself be enough to justify a potential queer reading of *Lud-in-the Mist*, but I believe that there is also plenty of textual evidence to support such a reading. A reading which unites the novel's esotericism, its drug-induced altered states, and its concluding vision of an integration of transgressive desires into heteronormative society. That transgressive desires are the novel's subtext is signalled by the words of the book's opening epigraph, which is taken from one of Jane Harrison's scholarly studies of ancient Greek religion.[9]

> The Sirens stand, as it would seem, to the ancient and the modern, for the impulses in life as yet immoralised,[10] imperious longings, ecstasies, whether of love or art, or philosophy, magical voices called to a man from his 'Land of Hearts Desire', and to which if he hearken it may be that he will return no more – voices , too, which, whether a man sail by or stay to hearken, still sing on.[11]

Mirrlees' novel is also esoteric, in the sense that it carries a concealed message obvious only to the initiated. This fact is made clear by a warning to the reader, cunningly delivered only at the very end of the novel, that 'the Written Word is a Fairy, as mocking and elusive as Willy Wisp, speaking lying words to us in a feigned voice. So, let all readers of books take warning!'[12] Thus compelling the reader to consider how they may have been deceived and ponder what subtlety of meaning they may have missed on first reading. Mirrlees and Jane Ellen Harrison both enjoyed composing coded messages with 'multilingual puns and playfully obscure literary references.'[13]

In addition, an abiding theme of *Lud-in-the Mist* is that of pagan survivals, traces of an 'old religion', to be found in folklore, riddles, songs and ancient cultural artefacts, a popular notion of inter-war folkloric studies. Part of the novel's background is Harrison's professional interest in the initiation processes of ancient mystery cults, which she examined in her studies of Greek religion. In *Themis: A Study of the Social Origins of Greek Religion* Harrison describes the rites of Trophonios:

> … the transit from one state to another is … drastically enacted. After purification the suppliant goes down into a chasm, slips through a hole feet foremost, is swirled away, has a vision, comes back through the hole reversed. Without exaggeration, he may surely be said to have accomplished a rite de passage. In the rites of Trophonios we seem to see the thing presented pictorially, physically, geographically; the rites are, as M. van Gennep would say, preliminal, liminal, postliminal.[14]

This process of rebirth is echoed in the uterine imagery which occurs early in *Lud-in-the-Mist* in a description of walking down a garden path in which living branches have been intertwined to create a tunnel.

> You enter boldly enough, but very soon you find yourself wishing you had stayed outside ... And is the only exit that small round hole in the distance? Why, you will never be able to squeeze through that! You must turn back . . . too late! The spacious portal by which you entered has in its turn shrunk to a small round hole.[15]

This is only one example of the embodied feminine to be found in Mirrlees's work, which is often expressed through the use of punning.

That *Lud-in-the Mist* is a novel of initiation is made clear by the title of the penultimate chapter, 'The Initiate', in which the novel's protagonist, Nathaniel Chanticleer, learns that he has been initiated into the Ancient Mysteries of Dorimare, by taking 'the vow made by the candidates for initiation into the first degree.' On which subject Mirrlees notes sagely, 'I doubt whether initiation ever brings happiness. It may be that the final secret revealed is a very bitter one ... or it may be that the final secret had not yet been revealed.'[16]

Regarding drugs and altered states in *Lud-in-the-Mist*, you know you're genuinely in drug territory when Nathaniel's wife complains of him smoking his 'green shag' other than in the pipe-room; 'you know how it always upsets me, Nat. I'm feeling quite squeamish this morning, the whole house reeks of it.'[17] In the context of the international female avant-garde of the 1920s, of which Mirrlees was an exponent by virtue of her work *Paris: A Poem* (1919), this recalls the notorious Dadaist performance artist and poet Baroness von Freytag-Loringhoven (1874–1927) who smoked hashish openly in her big china German pipe and wrote poems about her stoned perceptions.[18] But such hints are not really needed when the narrative of *Lud-in-the-Mist* revolves explicitly around a 'mysterious drug', namely fairy fruit. A moral panic ensues when fairy fruit smuggled into Dorimare from Fairyland is corrupting the youth of a Tolkienesque early modern fantasy realm. Those who fall under its influence experience altered states of consciousness and run off to Fairyland, a realm from which none are expected to return. Rumours concerning fairy fruit and its influence reach the town of Lud-in-the-Mist as 'madness, suicide, orgiastic dances, and wild doings under the moon' and 'the more they ate the more they wanted.'[19]

Referred to just once as a 'mysterious drug', under the rule of an earlier aristocratic regime fairy food was originally a sacrament reserved for the priestly class of the 'old religion'. A sacrament which 'had always been connected with poetry and visions.'[20] Harrison was one of the early proposers of an ancient goddess-worshipping matriarchal culture, which was overcome by the arrival of a later patriarchal order dominated by male gods headed by Zeus. While Harrison does not, to my knowledge, propose a role for psychoactive drugs in initiation into Greek mystery cults, she would certainly have been aware that this was described by her mentor, the Classicist Erwin Rohde (1845–1898). He discussed such practices at some length in his book *Psyche: Seelencult und Unsterblichkeitsglaube der Griechen* (1890/1894).[21] Rohde was a significant influence on Harrison's interest in the ecstatic aspects of ancient Greek religion, whose book she reviewed for *The Classical Review*.[22] According to Rohde: 'The ancients were quite familiar with the practice of inhaling aromatic smoke to produce religious hallucinations.'[23]

Two hundred years before the era depicted in the novel, the aristocratic regime in which fairy fruit was a sacrament had been overturned in a revolution. Under the new ruling class of prosaically minded merchants, fairy fruit became anathema. To eat fairy fruit was then regarded as a 'loathsome and filthy vice, practised in low taverns by disreputable and insignificant people.'[24] Fairy fruit was such an abomination under the new regime that the laws banning its consumption and importation even refused to refer to it by name. Instead, it was referred to in law by the euphemism 'woven silk', a riddle to which I will return.

In *Lud-in-the-Mist*, altered states are invoked by eating fairy fruit or simply by the approach to Fairyland through the Debatable Hills. As the novel's protagonist Nathaniel Chanticleer climbs these hills which form the liminal border with Fairyland, intent on rescuing his son—a victim of fairy food—things get progressively stranger. "'But it isn't real, it isn't real,' he muttered. "I'm inventing it all myself. And so, whatever happens, I shan't mind, because it isn't real'" suggesting some knowledge, on Mirrlees' part, of navigating altered states.

> It was growing dark. He knew that he was being followed by one of the stone beggars, who had turned into a four-footed animal called Portunus. In one sense the animal was a protection, in another a menace, and he knew that in summoning him he must be very careful to use the correct ritual formulary.[25]

Although conceived in a city that earned the soubriquet 'Paris Lesbos' due to its resident sapphic literary coterie, there are no overt sapphic references in the *Lud-in-the-Mist*. However, Mirrlees's earlier novel *Madeleine* (1919) was a novel of sapphic infatuation set in the literary salons of 17th century Paris. *Madeleine* was judged by Virginia Woolf to be a *roman-à-clef*, 'all Sapphism as far as I've got – her [Hope Mirrlees] and Jane [Harrison].'[26] Mirrlees is still known principally for *Lud-in-the-Mist*, but she is now gaining attention as a significant modernist author on the strength of her short modernist work *Paris: A Poem* (1919). Sapphic aspects in *Paris: A Poem* were identified by the late Virginia Woolf scholar Julia Briggs, as well as several drug references. Briggs was brave enough to suggest that the poem's 'hallucinatory moments may be drug induced.'[27] Joannou's study of modernist literature (2013) describes the poem as 'resolutely sensual' and that it may be a coded love letter from Mirrlees to Harrison. It combines *fin de siècle* decadence with its references to hashish, absinthe and Verlaine, with a modernist use of typefaces reminiscent of Apollinaire's poems in his collection *Calligrammes* (1918), published the year before *Paris: A Poem*.

To suggest that the corrupting influence of fairy fruit points towards Fairyland being an emblem of sapphic culture based simply on 'fairy' as an already extant epithet for a homosexual, might seem over-interpretive. However, several characters in the novel are typified as 'queer', another then contemporary term for male or female homosexuality, and the context in which the term is used suggests something more than meaning strange or odd. Nathaniel Chanticleer pondering his relationship with another character feels for a moment 'as if he really loved the queer, sharp-tongued, little upstart.'[28] By return, the other remarks 'I have sometimes had the impression that (you were) well, a whimsical fellow, given to queer fancies.'[29] While these characters are male, the use of male homosexual figures to represent sapphic homosexual affections, was in fact quite common in the 1920s. Radcliffe Hall's novel *The Well of Loneliness* (1928), a direct plea for recognition of the normality of a sapphic orientation, was judged obscene and banned by a British court because it defended 'unnatural practices between women'.[30] Writers such as Vita Sackville-West and Violet Trefusis veiled their sapphic affairs by substituting male personae for female figures in their autobiographical novels *Challenge* (1923) and *Broderie Anglaise* (1935).

What then of an argument for 'fairy food' as a coded emblem of same-sex relations, when any youth who falls under the influence of such a 'loathsome and filthy vice' or is 'to be suspected of such a thing … [can expect] complete social ostracism'?[31] Well, these are terms which in any other contemporary context would refer to same-sex relations, and sapphism and drug use were intimately associated in bohemian *fin-de-siècle* Parisian culture. According to Nicole Albert, 'in the turn-of-the-century imagination, sapphic pleasures were inevitably linked to drugs', and she quotes a critic in the journal *Fantasia* who asserts that 'Sapphism goes hand in hand with opium and (cocaine).'[32] For Mirrlees, after three years in Paris Lesbos the association of the homoerotic and drug use would have come naturally. When in Paris, Mirrlees and Harrison used to tend the grave of Baudelaire in the cemetery of Montparnasse.[33] Baudelaire originally proposed *Les Lesbiennes* as the title for his collected poems, which was eventually published as *Les Fleurs du Mal* (1857).[34] Then there is also the curious legal euphemism of 'woven silk' employed by the narrow-minded burghers of Dorimare to refer to 'fairy fruit'. Well, woven silk is the fabric Satin, and 'a Satin' was established Parisian slang for a lesbian, based on the lesbian character called Satin in Zola's novel *Nana* (1880). This piece of *argot* was well enough known to be included in an 1895 handy German dictionary of Parisian slang, which simply lists 'Satin = Lesbienne, after the name of a person in Zola's *Nana*' (1880).[35] All of which is enough to establish that in the desire for and indulgence in fairy fruit, Mirrlees was painting, at least in part, a veiled narrative of those 'imperious longings as yet immoralised' of same-sex love, and co-identifies such longings with an altered state of consciousness which 'had always been connected with poetry and visions.'[36]

The Debatable Hills, the liminal zone between Fairyland and the fantasy realm of Dorimare, is a border which Mirrlees may or may not have transgressed physically herself, as she writes in one of her later poems 'Et in Arcadia Ego':

> I have no wish to eat forbidden fruit,
> I did not gather roses when I might,
> Now I am old and cold,
> The years begin to turn on me and bite.
> …
> I can watch the droves of little singing maids
> (They are so close, just out of reach!)
> Tuning Aeolian lyres upon the Lesbian beach[37]

The singing maids of the Lesbian beach are the self-same Sirens of the epigraph taken from Harrison in which they represent 'impulses in life as yet immoralised, imperious longings, ecstasies, whether of love or art, or philosophy … calling to a man from his "Land of Heart's desire".'

Mirrlees depicts in these lines her regrets at failing to engage with the sapphic milieu she had encountered as deeply as she might have wished, either romantically or physically. Perhaps she feels that she missed the opportunity to enjoy the physically erotic aspects of a sapphic inclination when she was younger. She was certainly capable of a bold sensuality, albeit veiled in clever punning, where a character in her earlier novel *The Counterplot* (1924) says 'A lady can be dated by the fact of whether it's the *Blue Danube*, or the *Sourire d'Avril*, or the *Merry Widow*, that glazes her eyes and parts her lips ... when in a deliciously artificial atmosphere sex expands and, like some cunning hunted insect, makes itself look like a flower.'[38]

Lud-in-the-Mist, with its allusions to magic, drug-induced altered states, and a veiled sapphic subtext, concludes with the inhabitants of Fairyland finally being welcomed back into Dorimare society. This is a vision of the integration of same sex relations into mainstream society, but one that could escape public censure, only being understood by those 'in the know'. An early 20th century satirical popular song[39] described the home of New York's gay community 'the intermediate sexes', in the line 'Fairyland's not far from Washington Square', Washington Square being next to bohemian Greenwich Village, already in the 1920s a haven for all kinds of counterculture.[40]

Fairyland in *Lud-in-the-Mist* is a trope for the Other, a forbidden transgressive realm nearby, but accessible only by crossing a dangerous liminal border. That realm is associated with an altered form of consciousness 'connected with poetry and visions', an alternative ecstatic form of consciousness achieved by initiation. The idea that a homoerotic/homosocial orientation is associated with the possession of creative talents by a person was proposed by Edward Carpenter (1844–1929), whose *The Intermediate Sex* (1908) argued that homosexuality was a natural and increasing orientation for a portion of human society, with which Mirrlees may well have been familiar. Carpenter's writings sought to counteract negative images of same-sex orientation and interpret it as an emotional or spiritual rather than purely physical orientation. Mirrlees's novel points to an alternative way of knowing and being, represented by a rejected class of society imbued with a radical otherness—a sapphic way of knowing of a sisterhood, such as that envisaged by Natalie Barney (1876–1972) who had planned to create a colony of female poets on the Greek island of Lesbos in memory of its former inhabitant the Greek poet Sappho (c. 630–c. 570 BC). Harrison wrote that 'If I had been rich I should have founded a learned community for women, with vows of consecration and a beautiful rule and habit.'[41]

Notes

1   For example, the Ballantine edition of *The World's Desire* (1972) by H. Rider Haggard and Andrew Lang used *Astral Body Asleep* by psychedelic artist Abdul Mati Klarwein for its cover.

2   Mirrlees 2018: 117. '…the Senate were beginning to congratulate themselves on having at last destroyed the evil that for centuries had menaced their country, when Mumchance discovered in one day three people clearly under the influence of the mysterious drug and with their mouth and hands stained with strangely coloured juices.'

3   Gaiman 2002: 78

4   Neil Gaiman in Swanwick 1999: *v*

5   I have used the term sapphism, as used here by Mary Beard, throughout this paper to refer to female homoerotic and homosocial culture. This is because this was a term current in the 1920s when Mirrlees was writing and is thus representative of how that culture conceived of itself and was represented.

6   A role-call of the lesbian literary 'ladies of the Left Bank'.

7   Beard, 2022: 139

8   Ibid.: 213: n.7

9   Harrison 1908

10   In Jane Ellen Harrison's *Prolegomena*, 'unmoralized', in Mirrlees epigram (1926) 'immoralised'. In the   Gollanz paperback editions (2000/2008/2018) it is rendered in error as 'immortalised', which completely loses the intended sense. Definition of immoralize: 'to make immoral' https://www.merriam-webster.com/dictionary/immoralize, thus the epigram refers to the impulses in life until now branded immoral.

11   Harrison, 1908: 206

12   Mirrlees, 2018: 264

13   Beard 2002: 136

14   Harrison, 1912: 510

15   Mirrlees 2018: 3

16   Ibid.: 260

17   Ibid.: 143

18   Horowitz & Palmer 2000: 94

19   Mirrlees 2018: 16

20   Mirrlees 2018: 11

21   'Psyche: The cult of the soul and the belief in immortality of the Greeks'

22   Harrison 1890/94

23   Rohde 1925: 273, n.39

24   Mirrlees 2018: 15

25   Ibid.: 241

26   Vanita 2006: 93

27   Briggs 2006: 87

28   Mirrlees 2018: 42

29   Ibid.: 43

30   Hilliard 2021: 42

31   Mirlees 2018: 15

32   Albert 2017: 198

33   Mirrlees 2018: xiv

34   Leakey 1992. 3

35   Villatte 1895: 264

36   Mirrlees 2018: 11

37   Mirrlees, Parmar 2011: 27

38   Mirrlees 1924: 132

39   This satirical ditty was composed by Robert Edwards, who performed as a novelty act with ukulele, and described the association of New York bohemians with same sex culture with the lines 'Way down south in Greenwich Village/In the Freud and Jung and Brill age/People come with paralysis/For the balm of psychoanalysis /Here the modernist complexes /And the intermediate sexes/ – Fairyland's not far from Washington Square'. *The Greenwich Village Epic* from Edwards, R. (1917). *The Song Book of Robert Edwards: Troubadour of Greenwich Village*. New York: The Knickerbocker Press. Qtd. in Watson 1993

40   Faderman 1992: 168. 'Greenwich Village which in the 1920s had been a melting pot of all manner of gay and straight people'.

41   Harrison 1925: 89

4

The Altered States of David Lindsay

Three Psychedelic Novels of the 1920s

The novels of the Scottish author David Lindsay (1876–1945) were originally published with moderate success in the 1920s and '30s and employed elements of the fantastic and occult. However, Lindsay quickly became a forgotten figure in literature until the least successful of his novels, an extraordinary and elaborate fantasy *A Voyage to Arcturus* (1920) was later republished by Gollancz.[1] It went on to be published in numerous popular paperback editions, thereafter becoming something of an underground classic during the psychedelic 1960s and '70s, along with the work of other rediscovered fantasy authors such as Mervyn Peake, Lord Dunsany and JRR Tolkien.[2]

Notwithstanding the observation of Fortean author and fringe culture pundit Mark Pilkington that *Arcturus* might well be 'the most psychedelic novel ever written',[3] and the fact that Rick Doblin, founder and executive director of the psychedelic campaigning organisation

MAPS, named the home he built *Arcturus* in honour of Lindsay's book,[4] the role of the consumption of psychoactive substances in the narrative of *Arcturus* seems to have gone almost entirely unremarked in the critical literature.[5]

The failure to incorporate psychedelic aspects of *Arcturus* in critical evaluations of Lindsay's work is probably for three reasons. Firstly, the references in *Arcturus* to eating and drinking followed by altered states of consciousness are easily read over unnoticed within the overall fantastic context. Secondly, the one novel of Lindsay's that explicitly involves the ingestion of a psychoactive drug, *The Violet Apple*, was written in 1924 but remained unpublished until 1976,[6] and even then has remained hard to find and expensive to purchase second-hand. Thirdly, there is the ignorance, and perhaps prudery, of literary commentators concerning matters relating to the use of psychoactive drugs, when their focus on the work is otherwise.

The one scholarly exception is David Sellin's book length study of Lindsay in which he observes that the 'gnawl water' that flows on the planet Tormance in *Arcturus* 'transforms sometimes insidiously, and sometimes brutally, the entire personality, like a powerful drug.'[7] The water produces a curious effect on the principal character named Maskull. 'Sometimes the water acts upon his senses to intoxicate him, as if Tormance did not signify a land of torments but delights. Sometimes in contact with the water, he receives an electric charge which stimulates him.'[8] According to Sellin, the water flows from Crystalman, a demiurgic figure, and 'intoxicates the better to deceive… It appears to be a source of life, but the life it offers is that of Arcturus which means in Lindsay's eyes a certain form of death.'[9] In Sellin's understanding, for Lindsay the seductive powers of beauty, art, love, and the will to live, are all illusions to be overcome. The means of overcoming them is the pursuit of pain and 'gnawl water' merely serves to enhance the illusory glamour of the material world.

As an authorial debut, *Arcturus* was not a success. Of 1,430 copies that were printed fewer than 596 were sold.[10] However, it was amongst the first works of the early 20th century writers of fantastic fiction to be rediscovered during the science fiction and fantasy boom of the 1960s and '70s. More recently in 2002, a fine collector's edition was published by Savoy Books with an introductory essay by acclaimed graphic novelist Alan Moore. Lindsay's own title for his novel was the fungally suggestive 'Nightspore on Tormance', but it was retitled *A Voyage to Arcturus* on the advice of the original publishers. Tormance, carrying a combined sense of both torment and romance, is one of many curious portmanteau words used by Lindsay in *Arcturus* for the names of characters and places. Following the failure of *Arcturus* to sell, Lindsay turned to expressing his interest in altered mind-states in novels of domestic drama in country houses set among the 'anyone for tennis' upper middle classes of the interwar period.

Arcturus is perhaps best described as a science fiction picaresque in which a human named Maskull visits a distant planet, and encounters several of its inhabitants. Each of these varied inhabitants lives in a different realm and represents a different philosophy, which in turn Maskull rejects, murdering two of these alien persons by his own hand. It should be emphasised that *Arcturus* is not a pleasant read, containing many violent scenes. There are nine deaths in total, four of which are killings and the other five are in one way or another consequential upon the actions of others and the progression of the story. Eventually Maskull achieves an apotheosis in which the illusory nature of the material world becomes clear. In this state it is revealed how the loathsome glamour of the physical world is animated by the spirit trapped within it.

This spiritual energy is called 'Muspel fire' and is envisioned as green atomic corpuscles whose 'fire had been abstracted, its cement was withdrawn, and, after being fouled and sweetened by the horrible sweetness of its host, broke into individuals which were the whirls of living will.'[11] The green atoms of this spiritual fire are forever striving to return to the point of their emanation, Muspel. In some individuals 'the green imprisoned life' was meagre while in others it was 'a hundred times greater'. Muspel fire is thus in eternal conflict with Crystalman (sometimes called Shaping), the evil master of the material world, who feeds on it for his own purposes. However,

> Muspel was no all-powerful universe, tolerating from pure indifference the existence side by side with it of another false world which had no right to be. Muspel was fighting for its life – against all that is most shameful and frightful – against sin masquerading as eternal beauty, against baseness masquerading as nature, against the Devil masquerading as God...[12]

Maskull dies in the process of his apotheosis but lives on in the person of an earlier, originally separate character, Nightspore. At the conclusion of the story, he joins Surtur, the personification of Muspel, who is also embodied in the human character Krag, in the eternal combat between spiritual and material realms. It is this struggle against Crystalman/Shaping, a Demiurge responsible for the material world, that earns *Arcturus* its reputation as a Gnostic novel.

The extraordinary inventiveness of Lindsay's *Arcturus*, which has made it justly famous, overcame the generally leaden prose of his writing that makes the tortuous tales of romantic and domestic intrigues of his later novels *The Haunted Woman* (1922), *Sphinx* (1923), and *The Violet Apple* (1924/1976) hard going, although they are not without a certain charm. Despite the clumsiness of his writing, *Arcturus* has gained the admiration of several other important authors, including CS Lewis (1898–1963), the literary critic and Yale Professor of Humanities Harold Bloom (1930–2019) and the well-known writer on the occult and paranormal Colin Wilson (1931–2013). While rejecting its philosophy, CS Lewis found in Lindsay's *Arcturus* a method of writing that informed the Christian 'theological science fiction' of his Space Trilogy that commenced with *Out of the Silent Planet* (1938). He described Lindsay as 'the real father of my planet books'.[13] According to Bloom 'Lindsay's uncanny nightmare of a book survives its dreadful writing'[14] and Bloom found what he considered the Gnostic vision of

Arcturus so compelling that he attempted his own explicitly Gnostic version on the same themes in the shape of *The Flight to Lucifer* (1979). Likewise, Colin Wilson also developed something of an obsession with Lindsay and *Arcturus*, penning more than half-a-dozen pieces on Lindsay in the form of essays, introductions, and also as editor and contributor to compendiums of works about Lindsay and in particular about *Arcturus*.[15]

Turning now to the mechanics of the novel *Arcturus*, we find that altered states are induced when the human visitor Maskull eats or drinks various substances found on a planet revolving around the star Arcturus. Here are two examples of the induction of altered states, the first by something drunk, the second by something eaten.

> When his own turn came to drink, he found the juice of the tree somewhat like coconut milk, but intoxicating. It was a new sort of intoxication, however, for neither his will nor his emotions were excited but only his intellect – and that only in a certain way. His thoughts and images were not freed and loosened, but on the contrary kept labouring and swelling painfully, until they reached the full beauty of an apercu, which would then flame up in his consciousness, burst and vanish. After that, the whole process started again.[16]

And...

> Maskull bit into the root. It was white and hard; its white sap was bleeding. It had no taste, but after eating it, he experienced a change of perception. The landscape, without alteration of light or outline, became several degrees more stern and sacred. When he looked at Corpang he was impressed by his look of Gothic awfulness, but the perplexed expression was still in his eyes.[17]

It must surely be difficult to believe that anyone who has a familiarity with the experience of psychedelic drugs would read these passages without identifying them as typical of experiences produced under the influence of such substances. The detail is such that they appear likely authored by someone who has had the benefit of such experiences himself. Whilst they could be derived from written descriptions available to Lindsay, their subtlety belies this. Either way, the process of the character's spiritual journey on the planet of Tormance proceeds partly by virtue of these experiences of altered consciousness. No doubt the Hippie readers of the battered cheap paperback reprints of *Arcturus* that lay around Sixties crash-pads read these passages with an appreciative murmur.

In Chapter 6 of *Arcturus* Joiwind introduces Maskull to the effects of 'gnawl water':

> He drank copiously. It affected his palate in a new way – with the purity and cleanness of water was combined the exhilaration of sparkling wine, raising his spirits – but somehow the intoxication brought out his better nature, and not his lower… Maskull now realised his environment as it were for the first time. All his sense organs started to show him beauties and wonders he had not hitherto suspected.[18]

However, it must be understood that the chapters and persons that Maskull meets on his journey represent various philosophies, each of which Maskull in turn rejects, and Joiwind turns out to be an innocent worshipper of 'Shaping', another name for Crystalman the evil Demiurge of material creation.

Regardless of the specific role played by psychoactive substances in *Arcturus*, it is curious that the extensive published commentary on the varied philosophical ideas contained in *Arcturus* largely fails to highlight the altered states induced by psychoactive substances found on Tormance or relate them to the explicit role played by psychoactive drugs in Lindsay's *The Violet Apple*. Even though Alan Moore observes in his

Introduction to the Savoy Books edition (2002) that 'Commencing with a séance, a conventional enough device in the fantastic stories of that period, the tale then turns into a kind of mescaline-fuelled picaresque', he fails to comment on the clear references to the consumption of mind-altering substances in the text.

Lindsay's second novel, *The Haunted Woman* (1922), takes the form of a drama of romantic intrigue and misunderstanding that is typical of his later work. In it, a set of secret rooms in an ancient house provides a view into an alternative medieval world through an upstairs window, but the stairs to the rooms are only visible to those with a natural psychic perception. Intriguingly, visits to the room are entirely forgotten afterwards, leaving a sense of lost time. 'What kind of rooms could they be which had the effect of drugging the brain to permanent forgetfulness?' asks the central character Isabel. 'It was something in that house... It was like the call of a drug; she was a drug-maniac...'[19] Isabel has a number of romantic liaisons with the owner of the house conducted in the secret rooms, of which they both have only vague intimations afterwards, and they devise a plan to see if they really are meeting each other in this alternative reality.

In the case of Lindsay's third novel *Sphinx* (1923) an altered state is produced by playing back, in the mind of a waking person, recordings of other people's dreams. These are created by a sensitive device with something like a photographic emulsion, constructed by the main character. However, the experience of reliving another person's dream, as described in the novel, has a distinctly psychedelic feel. This excerpt is from a chapter suggestively entitled 'Evelyn is Initiated':

> Suddenly Evelyn was in the middle of a nightmare! The room streaming with sunlight, the open window with its blind only half lowered, the glorious green, blue, and golden world outside, the sweltering heat – all, without warning, had given place to a mad fantastic dream, into which she had not even time to wonder how she had fallen. She was not frightened, but it seemed to her as if nature had parted from its moorings and that she had somehow become transported into chaos!

The world in which she now was bore much the same resemblance to the ordered world of reality as a cubist painting to an actual scene or group of persons. It was a kaleidoscope of colours and sounds, odours and skin sensations. Everything was accompanied in her by such a variety and rapidity of emotion that she had scarcely the ability to realise her internal feelings at all. She was just one big *nerve*! … all was hopelessly mixed together – darkness and brightness, heat and coolness, one landscape and another, triumph, gloom, laughter, exaltation, grief. … the things only came in vivid hints and momentary splashes, immediately to be lost again. It was no dream, but the dream of a dream. Supposing reality to be solid and dreaming fluid, this was gaseous. The elements of life were in a condition of disintegration. They still existed, but in combinations so impossible that she could not even understand their meaning…[20]

If, as appears uncannily likely, David Lindsay had personal experience of psychoactive drugs, it looks as though he drew on such for this dream sequence. The use of psychoactive drugs in a fictional setting was hardly unique to the late 19th and early 20th century; consider for example the drug stories of HG Wells.[21] So, incorporating the effects of a psychoactive drug into fiction would not make Lindsay unique in terms of his era. I have, however, found nothing in the commentary on Lindsay's works or his biographical details that indicates his personal use of psychoactive drugs. Between 1913 and 1917 Aleister Crowley was holding regular Anhalonium parties, at which he dispensed an extract of peyote to figures from the occult and literary circles of the day,[22] though I have not been able to find any point of social contact between Lindsay and that milieu. Anhalonium as a recreational drug in the 1920s was well enough known for Cecil Gray, writing about contemporary classical music, to reference its use:

As a kind of drug, no doubt Scriabin's music has certain significance, but it is wholly superfluous. We already have cocaine, morphine, hashish, heroin, anhalonium, and innumerable similar productions, to say nothing of alcohol. Surely that is enough.[23]

In 1919 Lindsay moved to Cornwall, a move made by several writers and occultists during and after the First World War, such as DH Lawrence, the composer and occultist Peter Warlock, as well as individuals from Crowley's circle such as the author Mary Butts,[24] and the aforementioned Cecil Gray, biographer of Peter Warlock.[25] They were attracted by a sense of lingering paganisms, the wildness of the country and the presence there of mysterious megaliths.[26]

All of the psychedelic passages that I have quoted from Lindsay's novels could of course have been the product of Lindsay's imagination or culled from accounts by other persons. However, there is one further prompt to seriously consider whether Lindsay did have personal experience of psychoactive drugs. This is Lindsay's description of the experience of the explicitly psychoactive plant drug that plays a key role in his posthumously published novel *The Violet Apple*.[27]

In *The Violet Apple* the protagonist Anthony Kerr receives an heirloom: a seed claimed to come from the Tree of the Knowledge of Good and Evil in the Garden of Eden, which is held inside a glass ornament in the shape of a serpent. This heirloom is said to have been brought back from the Middle East by a crusader knight in the Middle Ages. Stories featuring secret knowledge learned in the Holy Land and brought back to Europe by crusader knights have been popularised by the novels of Dan Brown, who relied heavily on the cult work of pseudohistory *The Holy Blood and the Holy Grail*[28] for the notion of a secret stream of Gnostic heresy carried down through the ages. However, the authors of these books were themselves drawing on conspiracy theories that originated in the 18th and 19th century anti-Masonic literature that identified Freemasonry as the continuation of a centuries old stream of heretical gnosis which included the Templars.[29]

The glass container is accidentally broken and the seed gets to be planted and grows into a stunted little tree that produces two tiny violet apples, hence the title of the book. One of the apples is promptly eaten by Anthony's best friend's fiancée, an impetuous female character called Haidee. She then insists that Anthony eats the other remaining apple, reporting back to her on what he experiences before she reveals the nature of her own experience. On eating the second apple, Anthony undergoes a transformative experience during which he has a vision of Haidee as the spiritual embodiment of the female aspect of humanity and falls deeply in love with her.

In *The Violet Apple*, particularly accurate descriptions of the psychedelic experience form a compelling argument for Lindsay's personal experience of the effects of a psychoactive substance. The author describes the delayed onset and uncanny physical 'coming on' sensation after taking a psychedelic drug; the instinctive sense of the need to be left to oneself undisturbed for the duration; the shiver of fear that maybe you have taken a dangerous step combined with a need for something strong in reserve to take the edge off if things get too rough. After Anthony has chewed and swallowed his violet apple:

> The tang which still persisted in his mouth was rough, sharp, exquisite, bringing tears to his eyes by reason of its sweet acidity. Simultaneously, a long wave of voluptuous freshness continued to explore the passages and recesses of his interior like a summer breeze, and so far his exotic guest was retorting no movement of unfriendliness. But he was by no means reassured as yet; in fact, he could not be, for he was well aware that his experience was only just starting. And it was not so much his apprehension that made him uneasy, as some sort of actual voiceless, menacing physical response to his deed, creeping mysteriously upwards and outwards, hardly yet evident, but merely sensed by his instinct....
>
> He was glad he had not eaten that fruit at Croom, with his journey in front of him. He had the feeling of a wild beast which recognises the approach of sickness, and slinks away from its fellows into the remotest thicket it can find. He congratulated himself he had not advertised his return beforehand; his friends knew that he was away, and no-one would be likely to call. Anyway, he would see nobody. There was brandy in the cupboard, in case of need.[30]

However, having initially ingested the fruit, and after making every provision to be undisturbed, Anthony is interrupted by the arrival of his own (estranged) fiancée Grace, who is convinced that he is having an affair with the other consumer of the forbidden fruit, Haidee. The pain of having to entertain an unexpected and unwelcome visitor while high on a psychedelic, to whom you can't reveal your altered state, is depicted with an accuracy that is unerring to anyone who has had the same unfortunate experience. Grace arrives seeking a reconciliation following their estrangement due to her jealous suspicions concerning Anthony's relationship with Haidee. However, now under the influence of the 'violet apple', it is only Haidee, Eve to his Adam and confederate in transgression, that Anthony can think about.

> He wished he had not asked her up. It would have been better for her to find out *slowly* how that old life was ended for him – had no longer any meaning for him. He did not want her to be unhappy. She could not possibly understand his apotheosis.
>
> 'By God! That's a queer word.' He said, stopping short in his reflections, for it sounded to him as clear as if he had spoken it aloud. 'What apotheosis have I undergone? – and what am I talking about? What has changed within me the last half-dozen hours, that I should now be regarding it as quite settled that I am to part from Grace?'
>
> And then, as the door opened, and Grace herself entered the room alone and unannounced, the name HAIDEE appeared suddenly to traverse the whole sky-arch of his thoughts from end to end... Yet it was not as a beautiful woman that she was present with him. It was as if she represented for him unthinkable lofty, maternal protecting spiritual influence, so that he stood, not face to face with her as one person with another, but in a sort of atmosphere compounded of her being; an atmosphere as necessary to his new existence as air to mammals and water to fishes... And he recognised that that was the great and single idea which for several minutes back had been inhabiting his soul, and which he did not wish Grace to discover there, and profane by discovering...[31]

When Grace confronts the tripping Anthony over his supposed affair with Haidee it is unbearable 'Oh, ye gods! Oh, go! go! go! go!' groaned the playwright mentally – and when he clasped his forehead with his hand, there were beads of perspiration there ... "This is unendurable".'[32] Unsurprisingly the engagement is over and Anthony finally accepts his soul kinship with Haidee.

The two initiates, Anthony and Haidee, despite being promised in marriage to mutual friends, accept that they are destined to be together and, once shared, reflect on their psychedelic experience in an interesting fashion. Anthony considers the experience thus:

> A drug falsely stimulates my brain for a few hours and I am deceived into imagining that this artificial exaltation corresponds to something real. Therefore the cessation of so pathological a deception, far from being a matter for lament, is a matter for self-congratulation; and I am well out of it.[33]

They feel that the intensity of the experience has actually robbed the real world of some of its magic, but that they will have to strive to recover a permanent sensibility of the world's natural magic by dint of their own endeavour.

> I have brought nothing away except a deteriorated intellect and an awakening to the disagreeable consequences of my conduct during those few hours; which would also precisely be the effect of whiskey, or opium, or cocaine. So what I now have to do is to forget all that, in order to build up my life anew from a fresh start.[34]

However, the full picture is much more ambiguous, as Lindsay was almost certainly compromised by the negative perception that a positive outcome to a drug experience would have had in an era that included the publication of Aleister Crowley's *Diary of a Drug Fiend* (1922) and pulp drug tales such as David Garnett's *Dope Darling* (1919).[35] Although he designates the drug experience of the violet apple as 'artificial', the outcome is positive and when Anthony and Haidee meet to share their experience it is described in much more positive terms:

> A silence followed, not of embarrassment, but simply because neither had anything further to say immediately. And if the marvellous experiences from which all these changes had arisen remained unreferred to, that also was not on account of any delicate reluctance on the part of either to introduce an awkward topic. It merely meant that both felt that there was nothing to be said about it. The high sacred hour was past, and to analyse it, even between themselves, would be a profanation. It was always in their hearts.[36]

The narrative of *The Violet Apple* takes place in the few days leading up to Easter Sunday and Anthony and Haidee's psychedelic experience is finally framed, somewhat clumsily, within a Christian context. This is in strange contrast to the frequent understanding of Lindsay's religious or metaphysical outlook in *Arcturus* as being Gnostic. In addition, a possible key to understanding *Arcturus* is Lindsay's interest in the Norse mythology that found clear expression his final novel *Devil's Tor* (1932). Lindsay derived Muspel, the source of spiritual energy in *Arcturus*, from *Múspellsheimr* (the world of fire) in Norse mythology, and the name 'Surtur' from Surtr, the lord of *Múspellsheimr*. Alan Moore considered the metaphysics of *Arcturus* a personal Kabbalah of Lindsay's own contrivance, without obvious sources, though Nietzsche and Schopenhauer are regularly named as influences. Little biographical information is available suggesting what contacts Lindsay may have had with occult or literary circles. Though biographies state he met his wife at a literary club in 1916, according to Sellin 'Myers and Visiak seem to be the only two writers with whom Lindsay maintained any relationship.'[37] However, something caused him to abandon a career working for a Lloyd's Insurance Underwriter in the City at the age of about 40, and dedicate himself to writing and publishing *Arcturus* following his demobilisation in 1919, never having seen active service.

The sensitivity of Lindsay's descriptions of psychedelic type experiences stands in distinct contrast to the clumsy prose of the turgid dramas of the romantic entanglements of the 'anyone for tennis?' set, in which he contrived to set the fantastic elements of his stories following the initial financial and critical failure of *Arcturus*. However, these domestic comedies of errors composed of petty misunderstandings and deceptions do evidence Lindsay's belief in the near impossibility of effective human communication, especially where material issues such as wealth, status or conformity to social values are a determining factor. It is also possible that *The Violet Apple* contained significant biographical elements. The protagonist, a writer of light entertainments for the stage, dissatisfied with the vanity of his profession, determines to abandon it and move to the countryside just as Lindsay actually did. In *The Violet Apple*, after his transformative experience, Anthony declares to his sister that he's giving up writing for the stage and that instead he has 'thought of buying a small property in Devon or Cornwall, and developing it, as a recreation to keep the devils away.'[38]

Lindsay's novels all point to a 19th and early 20th century culture of altered states that remains relatively unexplored. As further metaphors of the extra perceptions bestowed by the ingestion of psychedelics, during his journey across Tormance Maskull's body grows a variety of bizarre new external sense organs with names such as the Poign, the Magn and the Sorb. The function of one pair is explained to him as 'probes', which 'are the gates opening into a new world' but in effect they 'had no independent function of their own, but only intensified and altered his other senses'[39] and whose purpose may thus be likened to the effects of psychoactive drugs.

Arcturus then should perhaps be reassessed, on the basis of its descriptions of altered states induced by eating or drinking, its additional organs of perception, and in the light of the explicitly psychedelic content of *The Violet Apple*, as an essentially psychedelic text.

Notes

1   *A Voyage to Arcturus* was republished first in 1946 by Gollancz and then again during the science fiction boom of the 1960s by Gollancz (UK) and MacMillan (US) in 1963.

2   See entry 'Ballantine Adult Fantasy Series' in Stableford 2005.

3   Pilkington 2009

4   MAPS 2009: 1

5   For a man considered a neglected author, there are a large number of secondary sources on Lindsay and his works. An extensive bibliography of works by and about Lindsay can be found at violetapple.org.uk.

6   See Lindsay 1976. A second hardback edition of *The Violet Apple* was published on its own by Sidgwick & Jackson in 1978.

7   Sellin 2008: 163

8   Ibid.

9   Ibid.

10 Wolfe 2007: 9

11 Lindsay 1998: 314

12 Ibid.: 301

13 Qtd. in Wolfe 2007: 7

14 Bloom 2005: 506

15 See http://www.violetapple.org.uk/works/articles.php

16 Lindsay 1998: 301

17 Ibid.: 224

18 Ibid.: 55

19 Lindsay 1987: 165

20 Lindsay 2019: 51

21 See for example his short stories: *The Purple Pileus* (1896) about the transformative effect of a psychoactive mushroom experience; *Under the Knife* (1896) which includes an out of body experience under anaesthesia; and *The New Accelerator* (1901) with a drug which massively slows the perception of time.

22　　See Everitt 2016

23　　Gray 1924: 159

24　　Mary Butts was a regular user of various drugs and a sometime student of Aleister Crowley. She settled at Sennen on the Penwith peninsula on the western tip of Cornwall in 1932.

25　　In the early 1920s Peter Warlock himself experimented with drugs. In Smith 1994, Warlock's biographer refers to his use of cannabis. In a letter to Cecil Gray, his friend and an earlier biographer, Warlock says that he had tracked own a certain 'Crowleyian compound' at a certain 'pharmaceutician' (sic) which he would bring to Gray on his next visit. That Crowleyian compound might well have been Anhalonium, the peyote extract available at that time, to which Cecil Gray refers.

26　　Newman 2009

27　　David Lindsay started writing *The Violet Apple* in February 1924 and finished it in July. His publisher John Long rejected it, so Lindsay revised it between March 1925 and February 1926. However, it remained unpublished throughout his life. It was not until 1976 that it was collected with the unfinished The Witch and published by the Chicago Review Press. See http://www.violetapple.org.uk/tva/index.php

28　　Baigent et al. 1982

29　　See, for example, Partner 1982

30　　Lindsay 1976: 187

31　　Ibid.: 189

32　　Ibid.: 191

33　　Ibid.: 243

34　　Ibid.

35　　David 'Bunny' Garnett (1892–1981) was a British writer who published a sensational novel titled *Dope-Darling: A Story of Cocaine* (1918) as Leda Burke. The book's central character was loosely based on Betty May. Born Betty Marlow Golding (1893–1955?), she was a British singer, dancer, and model, who was also associated with occultist Aleister Crowley. Garnett is better known as the author of the short novel *Lady into Fox* (1922) in which a young woman, with tragic results, suddenly turns into a fox while she and her husband are out walking in the woods.

36   Lindsay 1976: 247–248

37   Sellin 2008: 38–42. L H Myers (1881 – 1944), son of F W H Myers (1843–1901), a founder of the Society for Psychical Research, and EH Visiak (1878–1972).

38   Lindsay 1976: 246

39   Lindsay 1998: 136

.

5

Bicycle Day in Ritual, Myth and History

Bicycle Day as Ritual Observance

Every year, on April 19ᵗʰ, Bicycle Day is celebrated by devotees of the psychoactive drug lysergic acid diethylamide, commonly known as LSD. This date is the anniversary of Albert Hofmann's initial self-experiment with LSD in 1943, which revealed the full power of the chemical's psychoactive effects as he cycled home from his laboratory in Basel, Switzerland.[1] The commemoration of this anniversary as Bicycle Day was begun by Professor Tom Roberts in 1985 and it rightly celebrates the extraordinary impact that the LSD experience has had on the creative arts, the study of consciousness, and spiritual and religious practices.[2]

Bicycle Day is now an annual event of popular psychedelic culture. Visitors to Basel can join the celebrations by following the original route cycled by Albert Hofmann from Sandoz AG headquarters to the site of his former home in nearby Bottmingen, a journey of some 30 minutes by bike. Hofmann's home at the time of his bicycle trip was on Oberwilerstrasse in Bottmingen, a suburb of Basel in Switzerland. A memorial sign has been placed nearby at the entrance to a short alley leading from Oberwilerstrasse to Gustackerrain, which has been named 'Albert Hofmann-Rain'.[3] It reads:

> Albert Hofmann 11.1.1906 – 29.4.2008: Swiss chemist and discoverer of LSD. Lived and researched from 1941 to 1968 in Bottmingen, on Gustacker[4] (Oberwillerstrasse 41), where he discovered the hallucinogenic effects of LSD as part of a self-experiment.[5]

Anyone who wishes to visit Basel and follow Hofmann's Bicycle Day route for themselves can find a near equivalent, cyclist friendly, route posted to 'bikemap' a website for sharing favourite cycle routes.[6]

Hofmann has been sanctified as 'St. Albert' in the painting *St. Albert and the Psychedelic Revolution* (2006) by artist Alex Grey, indicating the mythic status accorded to him by those who venerate LSD as a psychedelic sacrament.[7] He is further iconised in Grey's *Albert Hofmann and the New Eleusis* (2017),[8] in which the chemist is depicted as the patriarch of a revival of the ancient Greek Eleusinian Mysteries. Hofmann hypothesised that the Eleusinian Mysteries involved drinking a hallucinogenic potion involving ergot, a parasitic fungus of rye and other grains from which LSD was synthesised.[9]

LSD devotees of all shades observe Bicycle Day in ritual celebrations, alone or communally, informally or at staged events, either in person or virtually.[10] No doubt some will celebrate, circumstances allowing, by taking a dose of LSD. Hofmann's mythic status has been iconised and commercialised through sew-on patches depicting Hofmann on his bike, and on T-shirts, coffee mugs and other widely available memorabilia. Brian Blomerth's recent graphic novel *Bicycle Day* (2019) illustrates the events of the original Bicycle Day in a style that recalls that of art director Hanz Edelmann in the Beatles' animated feature film *Yellow*

Submarine (1968), or the work of psychedelic artist Peter Max. The charm and storybook style of Blomwerth's illustrations anchor the story in the romance of the psychedelic Sixties, with an additional fairy-tale aspect.

Bicycle Day celebrations are imbued with a magical quality in which Albert Hofmann, steered by intuition and happy accident, became the founding father of a worldwide psychedelic movement. However, the more iconic a person or an event becomes the more likely it is that history will elide with myth in imaginative reconstruction. As 19th April 2020 approached, I pondered what other significant events may have occurred on that date. What was happening in the rest of the world on that day? And how did that bike ride fit in with them?

While those who celebrate Bicycle Day consider LSD something of an alchemical elixir, capable of healing the troubled mind, or even a troubled world, few of them are likely to be mapping the discovery of the extraordinary properties of LSD within the context of the Second World War (1939–1945), which was then raging across Europe. The popular vision of the original Bicycle Day appears as that of a mild-mannered research chemist becoming the unwitting initiate into the revelatory powers of LSD, on a sunny day in a peaceful neutral Switzerland, secluded from world conflict.

When I investigated what other significant events occurred on that day, the most striking for me was the Warsaw Ghetto Uprising.[11] The population of the Ghetto, some 300,000–400,000 persons, were the Jewish population of Warsaw and the surrounding areas who had been confined there by the Nazis, and who refused to surrender themselves when the Germans came to evacuate the Ghetto, demolish it and liquidate its inhabitants. The German army were surprised when they were met by armed resistance and initial attempts to secure the Ghetto by the SS and auxiliary forces failed. Unbeknown to the Nazis, weapons had been smuggled into the Ghetto and resistance units had been formed there. Realising that the Ghetto's captives were not going to give themselves up willingly, on the night of 18th April 1943, German forces including tanks and artillery surrounded them. The following day, SS-Brigadeführer Jürgen Stroop ordered the destruction of the Ghetto and the evacuation of the Jewish population of Warsaw, and others who had been shipped into the overcrowded Ghetto for the purpose of transportation to the death camps. 19th April 1943 was also the beginning of Passover that year and is commemorated in the title of Joe Kubert's moving graphic novel *Yossel April 19, 1943: A Story of the Warsaw Ghetto Uprising*. In it, Kubert imagines what his own experiences as a child in the Ghetto might have been, were it not for the fact that his parents had previously emigrated from Poland to the USA. The battle for control of the Ghetto continued until May 16th when the last of its inhabitants, including male and female resistance fighters, had been captured or killed, and the Ghetto was set on fire.

Stroop Report – Warsaw Ghetto Uprising. Public Domain

The destruction of the Ghetto gave rise to one of the most haunting photographs of the Second Word War, that of a terrified small boy walking with hands raised under the gaze of armed SS soldiers. This photograph was selected for *Time* magazine's 100 most influential photographic images of all time[12] and has a comparable iconic status to the one taken in April 1972 of Phan Thị Kim Phúc, the then nine-year-old Vietnamese girl, running down a road, stripped of her burning clothes after falling victim to a US 'friendly fire' napalm bomb.[13] The photograph of the Jewish boy in Warsaw, who was part of a crowd of Jewish people that had emerged from hiding in an underground bunker, comes from the Stroop Report, a finely-bound volume compiled by SS-Brigadeführer Stroop for the benefit of the SS chief Heinrich Himmler, to commemorate the evacuation, transport and liquidation of the occupants of the Warsaw Ghetto.

Indeed, when Bicycle Day is being celebrated it seems likely that some of the young adults in the United States involved in the celebrations are entirely unaware that six million Jews and other Nazi victims were killed in the Holocaust as, in 'a survey of adults 18–39, 23% said they believed the Holocaust was a myth, had been exaggerated or they weren't sure.' And 'one in eight (12%) said they had definitely not heard, or didn't think they had heard, about the Holocaust.'[14] So, some young people celebrating Bicycle Day on April 19th may be ignorant not merely of the Warsaw Ghetto Uprising, whose anniversary falls on that same day, but of the Holocaust itself.

What significance might an event such as the Warsaw Ghetto Uprising and the subsequent liquidation of the Ghetto and many of its inhabitants have for events in Switzerland almost a thousand miles distant? The fairy-tale vision of a young research chemist cycling while on LSD against a background of Swiss mountains is one cheerfully isolated from the horrors of the Second World War, which hardly represents the reality of Sandoz's situation at that time. Switzerland, despite its neutrality, was operating a wartime economy, surrounded as it was by the Axis powers of Germany and Italy. It was largely dependent on them for imports, and negotiated agreements allowed Switzerland to continue to trade with both the Allies and Axis powers throughout the war.[15] In the case of Nazi Germany this resulted in moral compromises on the part of Swiss companies including, as we shall see, Sandoz.

The Wartime Operations of Sandoz

Sandoz, the company that employed Hofmann and which is therefore irrevocably linked to LSD, did not exist in isolation from the European conflict. It might not be immediately evident that wartime would have any bearing on the Swiss chemical industry, but it was in fact a stimulus for drug research. As demand for dyes—the product on which the fortunes of Sandoz were founded—declined during the war, the demand for pharmaceuticals such as painkillers understandably increased. Swiss firms continued to trade with and operate in Nazi Germany, and Sandoz had factories in Nuremberg and Munich. Swiss companies, Sandoz among them, were the only major non-German dye and pharmaceutical-producing companies to own factories and operate in National Socialist Germany between 1933 and 1945.[16]

When the operations of Swiss firms during the Nazi era were reviewed by the Swiss Independent Commission of Experts, established to examine the role of Swiss corporations during Second World War, it turned out that Sandoz did not emerge blameless in its relations with the Nazi regime. Swiss companies were necessarily well informed about the situation in Germany and 'in 1942 Sandoz was fully informed about the "euthanasia" programme, i.e. the murder of handicapped people' and 'alongside the Wehrmacht, SS medical units also bought Ciba, Roche and Sandoz medicines.'[17] In fact two of the medicines prescribed for Hitler by his physician Dr Morell were manufactured by Sandoz at their Nuremberg factory, *Calcium Sandoz* and *Optalidon*, an analgesic and sedative.[18] As a curiosity of psychedelic lore, in 1944 Hitler was also prescribed Harmine, formerly known as Telepathine and Yageine, this latter name reflecting its isolation from *Banisteriopsis caapi* which forms the essential MAO component

Calcium Sandoz Nurnberg – from the author's collection

of the Amazonian psychedelic brew ayahuasca, also known as yagé. Harmine was being used at that time as a medication against Parkinsonism and Hitler was suffering from uncontrollable tremors.[19]

Swiss companies operating in Nazi Germany were put under pressure to 'Aryanise' their companies, in line with Nazi ideology, and purge them of all non-Aryan people. It did not take long for Sandoz and several other Swiss companies to adapt to the conditions in Germany after the Nazis took power. Sandoz reorganised its subsidiary in Nuremberg in early 1933, reducing its Swiss share capital to give it a more German character. The Jewish chairman of its board, Nobel prize winner Richard Willstätter, was persuaded to resign from his position. This resignation was encouraged by Arthur Stoll, director of Sandoz and a personal friend of Willstätter, his former teacher.[20] Though Stoll later helped Willstätter to escape from the Nazis to Switzerland, 'the relationship between the two men was permanently affected.'[21]

In recognition of their complicity with the Nazi regime, Novartis, the successor corporation to Ciba, Geigy and Sandoz, later made a solidarity contribution of 25 million Swiss francs to the settlement of claims from the Second World War. Novartis has also paid a contribution to the Foundation Initiative of German Business and the Austrian Reconciliation Fund, a total amount of around three million francs.[22]

Summarising the relationship of Swiss chemical companies with Nazi Germany, the Independent Commission of Experts report concluded:

> The companies' personnel policy indicates that in addition to business logic, decision-makers' ethical attitudes played a part in shaping corporate action in Nazi Germany and occupied Poland. Even so, the Swiss chemical companies continued trying to increase their turnover in Germany even after 1933, launching new products and tapping into a new customer base among the National Socialist authorities and Nazi Party organisations. Although the Swiss companies' decision-makers represented a wide range of political views, their corporate actions generally conformed in practical terms with the interests of the Nazi regime.[23]

However, any suggestion that during the war Sandoz was part of IG Farben, the German chemical industry cartel that was notorious for its use of slave labour, medical experiments on inmates at concentration camps, and for supplying the poison gas Zyklon B used in the gas chambers, is erroneous. The Swiss companies Sandoz, Ciba and Geigy had formed a Swiss cartel 'Basle A.G.' in 1918, which joined with German (IG Farben), French (Kuhlmann) and British (ICI) companies to form a quadripartite cartel, but this was necessarily dissolved at the onset of the Second World War.[24] Still, the moral standing of Sandoz was compromised by the business opportunities created by wartime demands for pharmaceuticals and personal relations within the company were strained through complicity with the implementation of the racial theories of the Nazi regime.

Einhorn, Willstätter, Stoll & Hofmann:
A Phytopharmaceutical Dynasty

Organic chemicals derived from natural sources have been used since ancient times as dyes, medicines and poisons, and with the development of organic chemistry in the 18th and 19th centuries, scientists sought to isolate their active principles and to synthesise them. At the time of his discovery of the properties of LSD, Hofmann was the heir to a phytopharmaceutical dynasty, one dedicated to the isolation and synthesis of the active principles of medicinal plants. So, I turn now to the academic, political, and cultural contexts of the persons involved in Sandoz, and the conditions in which the LSD discovery emerged. Unfortunately, we shall see that as well as corporate ethics being compromised by business interests, the academy and scientific reputation were no protection against race prejudice.

As well as that of Albert Hofmann, several other names are familiar to those who have taken more than a cursory interest in the history of LSD's discovery. None more so than the name of Arthur Stoll (1887–1971) under whose supervision Hofmann was working at the time. Stoll started work for Sandoz in 1917, recruited to head a new pharmaceutical department,[25] the same year that he was appointed professor of chemistry at the Ludwig Maximilian University of Munich.[26] He set to work immediately on identifying the active principals of 'pulva parturiens',[27] the preparation of raw ergot used by midwives to bring on childbirth or staunch post-partum haemorrhage.[28]

Before joining Sandoz, Stoll had spent eight years studying and working under Richard Willstätter,[29] and Willstätter's reputation must have been significant in securing Stoll's appointment at Sandoz. Willstätter won the Nobel Prize for Chemistry in 1915 for his work on elucidating the structure of plant pigments, including chlorophyll.[30] He dedicated his life to organic chemistry, and he had a profound interest in the chemistry of vegetable narcotics. His doctoral thesis under Alfred Einhorn (1856–1917), who had synthesised procaine, deduced the chemical structure of cocaine[31] and he continued his research into other plant alkaloids, synthesising several of them, and was the first person to synthesise cocaine. He also studied the properties of *Digitalis*, the Foxglove plant, working with atropine, hyoscyamine and scopolamine.[32] These were the alkaloids derived from plants long used in herbal medicine and considered to be the active ingredients of the so-called Witch's Ointments. Stoll continued Willstätter's studies of such anticholinergic agents in his own work on the cardiac glycosides.[33]

Working together, Stoll and Willstätter had perfected techniques in extracting and analysing the active agents in plant tissues from fresh and freeze-dried tissue rather than working from dry samples as had been the historical practice.[34] Ergot had been used first by midwives and later by male physicians to aid delivery by inducing uterine contractions, but dosage of crude

ALFRED EINHORN
Sc. D.

Alfred Einhorn 1856–1917.
Public Domain

extracts was problematic due to the varying proportions of active components. In 1918, Stoll succeeded in isolating a chemically pure ergot alkaloid; ergotamine. By isolating the active principles of ergot Stoll developed several pharmaceutical products such as Gynergen, which was effective due to its vasoconstrictive action in the treatment of both past-partum haemorrhage and migraine. In 1935 Hofmann, who had joined Sandoz in 1929 straight from university, requested that he be allowed to continue Stoll's work on ergot, although Stoll warned him of the difficulties involved.[35] However, in 1937 both men achieved the first partial synthesis of a natural ergot alkaloid, ergonovine.[36] Prior to his discovery of LSD, therefore, Hofmann stood at the end a long line of master and apprentice relationships in research concerning drugs derived from traditional plant medicines. These relationships were not immune to the political situation of Europe in the interwar years.

On 24th July 1924, Willstätter resigned his Professorship at Munich university as a gesture against the increasing effect of antisemitism in universities, which he believed was preventing the appointment of the best candidates to academic posts.[37] His account led to what has been called 'The Richard Willstätter Controversy', in which some of

William Willstatter 1872–1942. Public Domain from the collection of ETH-Bibliothek

Willstätter's colleagues, and later their descendants, accused him of overstating the case of antisemitism in academia.[38] Following his resignation, Willstätter retreated to the security and isolation of his home but continued remotely supervising work on his research interests by telephone.[39] Notwithstanding Willstätter's withdrawal into the world of privately supervised research, Sandoz, at the behest of Stoll, took him on to head the supervisory board of the Sandoz subsidiary in Nuremberg which was set up in 1926. Willstätter records 'So it came about that, now in my sixties, I wandered alone late at night once more through the quiet back streets [of Nuremberg] which were alive with memories.'[40]

Willstätter resisted the anti-Semitic restrictions progressively imposed by the Nazis and postponed the opportunity to escape from Nazi Germany until it became almost impossible to do so. He found himself unprotected by his prestigious academic status, as the Nazis were now closing in on Jews from all sections of society. Willstätter attempted a water crossing into Switzerland via a lake but was arrested and returned to Germany. Soon the Gestapo were actively searching for Willstätter, and he took to hiding in his garden when they came looking for him. The Swiss had by now cooperated with the Germans by stamping passports with a red J in an attempt to restrict the number of German Jews escaping to Switzerland. However, with Stoll's assistance, Willstätter eventually obtained a viable passport. He was therefore able to escape at last to Switzerland but had to leave behind his art collection and other valuables.[41]

Arthur Stoll and Richard Willstätter were not dedicated to science alone. They were clearly men of culture, heirs to a scientific revolution in which the arts, science and commerce were combined in a notion of cultural and social progress. In Stoll's words 'One of the most noteworthy endeavours of scientific research is to give the benefits of its splendid achievements to ever wider circles of the world's population.'[42] This is reflected in their personal commitments and interests outside of their careers in science. Willstätter was an enthusiastic art collector with a large collection of 19th and 20th century artworks and sculpture. It was comprised of hundreds of items, including works by Picasso, Cezanne and Van Gogh. Similarly, according to the American medical historian Chauncey D Leake, 'one of the greatest modern art collections was assembled by Arthur Stoll, brilliant director of Sandoz A.G. in Basel.'[43] Stoll's collection was published as *Sammlung Arthur Stoll. Skulpturen und Gemälde des 19. und 20. Jahrhunderts.*[44] According to an obituary, the collection 'centres round magnificent works by Hodler from each of his active periods. Stoll, however, did not merely collect, he actively helped many living artists by his collecting. He was also an active member of a Zurich and two Basle Art Commissions and a member of the Federal Art Commission.'[45]

One of the works originally owned by Stoll was eventually returned to family ownership under the recovery program of work looted by the Nazis from Jewish families. That painting was Gustave Courbet's work of 1876 'Entrée d'un

Arthur Stoll 1887–1971. Public Domain from the collection of ETH-Bibliothek

Gave' (Source of a Mountain Stream). It was seized in 1940/41 by the *Einsatzstab Reichsleiter Rosenberg* (ERR), the Nazi unit charged with identifying and seizing works of art for the Goering collection.[46] It was seized when they looted the extensive collections of Moïse Lévy de Benzion (1873–1943), an Egyptian department store owner, in Paris and at the family chateau 'La Folie' in Draviel, on the outskirts of Paris.[47] However, Goering's taste was for old masters and it was exchanged by the Swiss Fischer Gallery, notorious for dealing in Nazi plunder, for other looted items more to Goering's liking.[48]

The Swiss art dealer Theodore Fischer is infamous for the auctioning of 'degenerate art' seized by the Nazis and played a major role in the trade of artworks stolen by the German army throughout Europe. Fischer's gallery in Lucerne, Switzerland, sold the returned Courbet painting to Willi Raeber of Basel,[49] who in turn sold it to Galerie Rosengart of Lucerne, and then onto Arthur Stoll.[50] The painting was finally restituted by an order of 15th December 1948 to Paule-Juliette Lévy de Benzion, a relative of Levi de Benzion, the owner at the time it was seized by the Nazis.[51] There is a certain irony in that Courbet created the painting while living in political exile on Lake Geneva in

Switzerland and Stoll's friend Willstätter likewise became an exile with Stoll's assistance in a Swiss Hermitage overlooking Lake Locarno.

Arthur Stoll also became a close friend by correspondence of the author, poet and artist Hermann Hesse (1877–1962), whose art and writings he collected. This admiration was mutual and in a Festschrift for Stoll on the occasion of his seventieth birthday Hesse wrote 'That you, dear Jubilar, during your great lifework in the field of chemistry have not neglected music, painting, or poetry, but rather have devoted your love to them, may mean little to an only-a-chemist. To us artists it means much.'[52] Stoll's substantial collection of correspondence with Hesse, which were sometimes illustrated by Hesse, together with artistic and literary works are now in the Swiss Literary Archive in the *Hesse-Archiv* as 'Sammlung Stoll' (Stoll Collection).[53] Stoll had wide-ranging cultural interests and was described by Friedrich Bran at a Hesse Colloquium as 'den vielseitig gebildeten Chemie-Gewaltigen Arthur Stoll' (the multi-educated chemical giant Arthur Stoll).[54]

Stoll's grandson Dieter, writing about the relationship between Stoll and Hesse, explains how 'during a spa stay in Baden, a mutual acquaintance told (Hesse) in 1929 of new medications that Arthur Stoll had developed'.[55] Hesse then wrote to Stoll requesting a supply of a Sandoz product, Allisatin.[56]

Dieter Stoll reports that during their thirty-year pen friendship, the one thing which remained constant was Hesse's request for medication.[57] Stoll supplied him with medicines in return for books, paintings, and special printings.[58] Hesse's correspondence records that not only Stoll, but many other doctors and pharmacists supplied Hesse with the latest products with which he then experimented.[59] Hesse's son Heiner records the author's use of an opiate, which he took for eye pain for some years. 'He thus knew of the efficiency of this medicine probably not only as a pain reliever but also, through his experience, as a drug which would more easily penetrate into the subconscious, as he later described it in *Steppenwolf*.'[60]

Stoll's relationship with Hesse places him within the circle of Hesse's other friends such as Richard Wilhelm, translator of the Chinese divinatory work the *I Ching* and the classic Chinese Taoist text of inner alchemy *The Secret of the Golden Flower*, which were published with introductions by Wilhelm and Hesse's friend, the Swiss psychiatrist and psychoanalyst, Carl Jung. Hesse was also a friend of Hodler, many of whose paintings were in Stoll's collection, and several of which include women in the poses and *Lebensreform* costumes associated with modern dance. Hesse and Jung, among many other artists and writers, had a close association with Monte Verità, an early 20th century centre of utopian communitarian experiments and progressive creative arts and spirituality, at Ascona in Switzerland. It was also a centre of modern dance, the practices of which were often underpinned by esoteric notions of harmonising man and cosmos for the purpose of spiritual development, and from which Gurdjieff's Movements were derived.[61]

Stoll's close friendship with Hesse, and his collection of Hodler's work, place him in the flourishing inter-war cultural milieu of progressive arts, education and esoteric spirituality. It was in this context that the psychedelic properties of LSD first became known; and which may form part of the basis of Willis Harman's extravagant claims for the creation of LSD by members of an esoteric religious order, who were also employees of Sandoz, a theme to which I will return.

Bicycle Day Redux: History or Myth?

Returning to the subject of Bicycle Day itself, it was in the course of his work under Stoll's supervision that, according to Hofmann's account, he suffered an accidental 'laboratory intoxication' while working on compounds derived from ergot. Hofmann suspected the compound responsible was LSD-25, the twenty-fifth of a series of compounds previously synthesised and one which had been tested without any indication of useful properties. However, according to Hofmann's account he had an intuition that he should return to this compound and examine it again.

The discovery of LSD's extraordinary properties was thus the result of a series of extraordinary chance events. First, that Hofmann returned to a compound, LSD-25, previously tested and dismissed as being without useful properties, and second that Hofmann suffered a laboratory intoxication, despite the solid precautions exercised by an experienced chemist against such an eventuality when working with potentially toxic substances. On 19 April 1943, three days after his accidental intoxication, he tested his suspicion that LSD-25 was responsible and decided to take what he considered a cautiously small dose. The principal written source for the initial accidental intoxication and events of what has come to be called Bicycle Day is recorded in Hofmann's autobiography *LSD – Mein Sorgenkind* (1979),[62] though he must have told the story countless times both to conference audiences and individuals between 1943 and the writing of his autobiography.

Interestingly, Hofmann's account has been questioned on a number of bases, significantly by chemist, pharmacologist and world expert on psychedelic drugs Dr David E Nichols, in his paper 'Hypothesis on Albert Hofmann's Famous 1943 'Bicycle Day'' (2003).[63] Dr Nichols questions both the likelihood that Hofmann would pick just one out of a series of at least 25 compounds on a presentiment that something had been missed, and, that an experienced laboratory technician would suffer an accidental intoxication.[64] According to Dr Nichols 'the only hypothesis I can come up with that's consistent with all of these facts is that on April 16, 1943, Albert Hofmann did not get LSD in his body at all. He had a spontaneous mystical experience!', a spontaneous experience of the kind Hofmann records having had in his childhood.[65] Dr Nichols' conviction was so strong that 'when I saw Albert in Basel a couple years ago, I presented that particular hypothesis to him and said, "What do you think?" He said, "It's entirely possible."'[66]

Further questions concerning Hofmann's account have been raised by cultural historian Mike Jay in his paper 'Bicycle Day Revisited'

(2018). Jay consulted Hofmann's original report for Sandoz, which is held in the chemist's personal archive at Bern University. He found that 'the 1943 report is quite different from the celebrated version in *LSD: My Problem Child.*' Hofmann took a dose of just 250 micrograms, 'the smallest dose he thought he might conceivably notice', according to Jay. Unaware that LSD is active at extremely low doses,[67] he could not have imagined that this was the kind of dose that would later be taken only by experienced devotees of the LSD experience, and which would send him on an explosive trip. Without any intimation of the effects of such a dose, his experiences as recorded in his original report are unsurprisingly entirely negative:

> dizziness, visual disturbance, the faces of those present seemed vividly coloured and grimacing; powerful motor disturbances, alternating with paralysis; my head, body and limbs all felt heavy, as if filled with metal; cramps in the calves, hands cold and without sensation; a metallic taste on the tongue; dry and constricted throat; a feeling of suffocation; confusion alternating with clear recognition of my situation, in which I felt outside myself as a neutral observer as I half-crazily cried or muttered indistinctly.[68]

In Hofmann's classic account he reports that, as the power of the effects lessened, 'I could begin to enjoy the unprecedented colours and plays of shapes that persisted behind my closed eyes',[69] but Jay notes that 'there's little of this in the original report, which mentions "sensory distortions" but describes the visions as "unpleasant, predominantly toxic-green and blue tones".' In his original report Hofmann concludes that the 'symptoms were very similar to those that might be observed in an overdose of an amphetamine-type stimulant such as Pervitin.'[70] It was only later experiments by Hofmann and his friends and colleagues at much lower doses that finally revealed the potential for pleasant hallucinatory experiences of exotic landscapes and colourful kaleidoscopic patterns.

While both Nichols and Jay have questioned the accuracy of Hofmann's later accounts of his accidental intoxication with LSD, Hofmann's original report still confirms the essential circumstances as described in *LSD My Problem Child*. Nonetheless, a conspiracy history of the origins of LSD has grown up around the remarks made by Willis Harman in a radio interview broadcast in 1976,[71] which have developed into a complex mythology in which ergot is a secret Gnostic psychoactive sacrament passed down through the centuries. Harman's motives for his unsupported assertions about LSD as the product of a research project by an esoteric cabal at Sandoz are unclear but may reflect an awareness of Stoll's closeness to Hermann Hesse. Harman's story deserves examination if only because of his academic status and connections with the elite of West Coast psychedelic society that had contact with Hofmann and therefore needs to be assessed in these contexts.

Harman (1918–1997) was an educator with a PhD in Electrical Engineering who taught at Stanford University, after working for General Electric and undertaking Navy service. Through contacts with US West Coast New Age and human potential movements, he became a campaigner for the development of enlightened business and economic practices.[72] Harman developed links to the West Coast elite psychedelic circles of Gerald Heard, Aldous Huxley and the notorious Captain Alfred M Hubbard. In an interview on Australian radio in 1977, Harman claimed that Hofmann was one of two members of a religious community, centred around the teachings of Rudolph Steiner, working at Sandoz.[73] He further claimed that LSD was developed as part of a plan initiated by that group in 1935 that 'set out deliberately to synthesize chemicals which were like natural vegetable substances, and which they were well aware had been used in all the world's major religious traditions down through the centuries' and that 'by 1938 they had synthesized psilocybin, LSD and about thirty other drugs.'[74] According to Harman, Hofmann had 'cooked up the newspaper story that everyone has heard now, about the accidental ingestion of LSD.' While Harman's claims are unverifiable and far-fetched, given his academic background it is reasonable to assume him to be a person of intellectual integrity.[75]

Why would Harman spin such a tall tale confusing the history of the development of LSD, some of which was patently inaccurate?[76] It is possible that they may be born out of an awareness of Stoll's closeness to Hermann Hesse and the unproven assumption by the psychedelic counterculture of the 1960s and '70s that Hesse's novel *Der Steppenwolf* (1927) must have been influenced by Hesse's experience of mescaline. However, Hesse scholars have concluded that there is no evidence that Hesse had experience of mescaline.[77] Timothy Leary approached German chemist Heinrich Klüver, whose *Mescal: The 'Divine' Plant and its Psychological Effects* was published in 1929, on this question. Klüver was by then teaching at Chicago University and responded:

> To my knowledge Hermann Hesse never took mescaline (I once raised this question in Switzerland). I do not know whether he even knew of the mescaline experiments going on under the direction of Beringer in Heidelberg. You know, of course, that Hesse (and his family) was intimately acquainted with the world and ideas of India. This no doubt has colored many scenes in his books.[78]

German mescaline researcher, Kurt Beringer, published *Der Meskalinrausch seine Geschichte und Erscheinungsweise* in 1927, the same year as Hesse's *Der Steppenwolf.* Hesse may at least have been aware of the contemporary research into mescaline through his interest in the latest pharmaceutical developments. In the literature of psychedelics Hesse has been repeatedly stated to have been a friend of Beringer, but I cannot find anything to substantiate this, and it appears to be one of those assertions repeated practically verbatim in different accounts with no primary source.[79]

Hofmann also expressed his interest in Hesse's works, which he could hardly have avoided learning about after working so long with

Arthur Stoll. In a 1976 interview Hofmann was asked whether Hesse or Jung ever showed an interest in his LSD discovery. Hofmann replied,

> I never met Hesse, but his books - especially *The Glass Bead Game* and *Steppenwolf* - have deeply interested me in connection with LSD research. It is possible that Hesse experimented with mescaline in the 1920s as some have supposed—I have no way of knowing. Outside of one brief meeting with Jung at an international congress of psychiatrists, I had no contact with him.[80]

Between Stoll's friendship with Hesse, and as a collector of his work, it is not beyond possibility that Willis Harman's mysterious Sandoz-based followers of Steiner were none other than Stoll and Hofmann, and the multiple drug developments of the Natural Products division of Sandoz the supposed multiple psychoactive drug discoveries. There may have been sufficient contact between Hofmann and the West Coast psychedelic elite for them to have known about what Timothy Leary refers to in his 1982 autobiography as an 'informal wisdom school' gathered around Hofmann,[81] which included Jünger and various Basel based esoterically inclined intellectuals, which I will discuss in more detail later. It is difficult under the circumstances to draw any other reasonable conclusion.

Picking up on Harman's claims, digital media pundit Mark Stahlman has posted on the internet his theory of an unbroken chain of transmission of secret, ergot-based, ritual mysticism from the ancient Greek Mysteries of Eleusis, via various 18th-century secret societies to the supposed esoterically inclined members of Sandoz staff.[82] Stahlman's account follows what Leon Surette calls the 'fantasy history' of an unbroken tradition of esoteric knowledge passed down through secret societies, originating in the masonic and anti-masonic literature of the 18th century.[83] In the 20th century this became a staple of modern occultism and turns up in the literary work of Ezra Pound, TS Eliot and WB Yeats,[84] and later in popular occult conspiracy thrillers such as those by Dan Brown. Stahlman and Harman suggest the involvement of occult circles involving the German poet Stefan George, or followers of Rudolf Steiner respectively.

Stahlman's development of Harman's claim that LSD and other psychedelics were developed as part of an occult plan to save the world via the psychedelic sacrament of a centuries-old secret society, preceded an awareness among the psychedelic community of a novel published in 1933 which curiously mirrored Stahlman's secret history. In Austrian author Leo Perutz's novel of 1933 *St. Petri-Schnee* (St Peter's Snow), a landowning Baron, living in the remote countryside, learned that ergot was the secret psychoactive sacrament of the Gnostics and ancient Graeco-Roman mystery religions, a secret handed down through history. The Baron determines to create a drug with which to incite a religious revival and reinstate the Holy Roman Empire, headed by a pretender from a lost bloodline, whom he had located. He employs a female biochemist to isolate the active principal of an ergot-type fungus to produce the drug. He then arranges to test it on the unwitting local peasant population with disastrous results. The extraordinarily detailed prophetic nature of the novel has been taken as supporting Willis Harman's claims for an earlier date for LSD's discovery as part of an esoteric endeavour.

Conspiracy theories aside, my own research shows that Perutz could have assembled the elements of his novel from a variety of then existing sources (See Piper 2013). However, one might question why Hofmann never, to my knowledge, acknowledges that it was hardly surprising that a derivative of ergot should prove to be psychoactive. Günter and Giger point out that the hallucinogenic effects of ergotism are not related to LSD-25 because raw ergot contains no LSD-25, as it is a synthetic derivative of ergot.[85] Nonetheless it seems reasonable to assume that Sandoz must have carefully studied the entire history of ergot, which should have suggested the potential for psychoactive effects of ergot derivatives because the symptoms of convulsive ergotism include hallucinatory states. Sandoz records in its 75-year Jubilee volume that their 'research on ergot had been vigorously prosecuted for forty-four years', in other words since 1917 when Stoll first set up the Sandoz pharmaceutical department.[86] The truth is that the discovery of LSD was not the product of a lucky accident, but an outcome of the determination of Stoll's department to derive every possible pharmaceutically useful substance from ergot, a fact that Hofmann emphasises himself: 'Time and again I hear or read that LSD was discovered by accident. This is only partly true. LSD came into being within a systematic research program.'[87]

Stoll, Hesse and the *Bundesroman*

If anyone within the small staff of the Sandoz Natural Products department fits the bill for Harman and Stahlman's theory of an esoterically inclined insider at Sandoz, it is Arthur Stoll. Stoll's fascination with the works of Hesse certainly indicates an affection for the world of the author's mystical imagination. Initiation by secret societies was an abiding theme of his major novels.[88] Indeed, they follow the established format of the *Bundesroman* or 'League Novel' of the 18th and 19th century, in which individuals are guided in their inner development by mysterious forces: a spiritual mentor as in *Demian* (1919) or a secret society such as 'The League' (Bund) in *Journey to the East* (1932).[89] These tropes are born out of the mythology of the secret societies of that earlier period and its literary expressions. A highpoint of the form was Goethe's *Wilhelm Meister's Apprenticeship* (1795–96) with its Tower Society. The *Bundesroman* was already a somewhat archaic form when Hesse adopted it for his novels, but he had been profoundly influenced by it as a literary genre from a young age.

In Hesse's *Journey to the East* the members of 'The League' are comprised of figures of fiction such as Don Quixote, or characters from his own works such as Klingsor from *Klingsors letzter Sommer* (1920); personages from history such as Albertus Magnus (1200–1280); and living individuals such as the artist Paul Klee (1879–1940). The

League, whose members journey not only across space but also time, constitutes an Invisible College into whose membership Hesse places both real and fictional people with whose spirit Hesse identifies. His election of these real and fictional cultural heroes into his secret society echoes both the attribution of various famous personages (including Victor Hugo, Claude Debussy and Jean Cocteau as Grand Masters of the secret society, the Priory of Sion, in the pseudo-historical work *The Holy Blood, The Holy Grail*[90]), and the false ascription of the authorship of popular medieval grimoires to figures such as Albertus Magnus, one of Hesse's 'elect' in *Journey to the East*.

There is a certain irony if Harman and Stahlman's undocumented claims of LSD as the product of a secret society are in fact an extravagant reworking of Stoll's fascination with the work of Hesse, whose *Bundesroman* novels describe individuals guided on their spiritual quest by a mysterious magus or secret society. Forty years later LSD was being promoted as an agent of spiritual discovery by Timothy Leary's organisation, the League for Spiritual Discovery (LSD), whose name certainly owed something to the League in *Journey to the East*. Interestingly, when Hesse's books became popular during the psychedelic '60s and '70s, Leary provided introductions to editions of *Journey to the East*.[91]

Hofmann, long before Leary became an LSD guru, sensed the mystical potential of the LSD experience, and found a mentor in the German author Ernst Jünger (1895–1998). According to Hofmann's account, inspired initially by Jünger's collection of surrealistic vignettes published as *Das Abenteuerliche Herz*[92]—which also features the theme of initiation into secret orders—Hofmann, anxious to contact him, sought Jünger out shortly after the end of the Second World War. Jünger's *The Adventurous Heart* (1929),[93] to which Hofmann returned many times ('for the last forty years I have taken this book up time and time again'),[94] owes much to the work of *fin-de-siecle* decadents with its images of torture gardens and acts of grotesque violence in sections such as 'The Cloister Church'[95] or 'The Black Knight'.[96] It features a magus figure named Nigromontanus, who expresses Jünger's imaginative depiction of the influence of hidden masters.

> Among the things Nigromontanus taught me was the certain existence among us of a select group of men who have long withdrawn from the libraries and from the dust of the public arena, who are at work in the innermost spaces, in the obscurest of Tibets.[97]

Further, 'he once spoke of certain features of the Magnetic Mountain, of spiritual centers of such repellent power that they were unapproachable by ordinary senses and more unknown than the dark side of the moon.'[98] Hofmann's account of his interest in Jünger makes it clear that it predates his discovery of the psychoactive effects of LSD.[99]

Regarding his admiration for Ernst Jünger, Hofmann records that,

> Radiance is the perfect term to express the influence that Ernst Jünger's literary work and personality have had on me. In the light of his perspective, which stereoscopically comprises the surfaces and depths of things, the world I knew took on a new, translucent splendour. That happened a long time before the discovery of LSD and before I came into personal contact with this author in connection with hallucinogenic drugs.[100]

In Jünger's own words, 'our highest aspiration must be the stereoscopic glance that grasps things in their more secret and dormant physicality.'[101] Neaman notes the debt owed by Jünger's stereoscopic method of perception, which informs the pages of *The Adventurous Heart,* to the 'poetic synesthesia' of the French symbolist poets,[102] a process which extends our perception of the commonplace to include a range of magical or esoteric meanings.[103] This system of analogical correspondences, especially through colour, is a theme that emerges in the thoughts of members of Hofmann's 'Occultic Network', as Karl Baier calls them in his keynote lecture at the ESSWE7 conference of 2019,[104] in which psychedelics were explored in a context that mixed esotericism and Eastern spirituality.[105] In the philosophy of Nigromontanus, the philosopher and magus figure who reoccurs in Jünger's writings, the motif of the interpenetration of surface and depth is thematised. Microcosmos and macrocosmos are connected through a cosmic harmony based on analogies, especially through the system of colours and their symbolic meanings, a topic that was also important to the members of this occult circle who were engaged in developing an alternative understanding of man's relationship with nature.

This Occultic Network was effectively a group of likeminded friends—artists, writers, scientists and philosophers—with an interest in the effects of the psychedelic drugs mescaline, psilocybin and LSD. Baier coins the term 'occultic' to describe this network and locates it somewhere between 'occultist', referring to those who identify as members of an actual occult order or tradition, and 'occulture', the popular culture that appropriates all kinds of occult, esoteric and other outsider themes. According to Baier, Hofmann's Occultic Network is a subgroup within Hofmann's network of close friends and collaborators, many of whom crossed the borders between art, science, philosophy and theology, but not all of whom partook of psychedelics.

The members of this group were too individualistic to identify with any specific occult or esoteric tradition but were interested in these cultural currents in relation to psychedelic experience. They certainly understood that their interests were countercultural and that this made them outsiders. Several members identified with the politics of the Conservative Revolution, a term coined by Armin Mohler (1920–2003) to describe the members of a radically conservative resistance to the enforced democracy of the Weimar Republic, of which Ernst Jünger and Carl Schmitt were prime representatives. Mohler worked as Jünger's secretary during the first phase of the operations of Hofmann's network but did not use any drugs. However, he was an important social networker, keeping the members in touch with arrangements. The close relationship between Hofmann and Jünger was at the core of this group. Other significant members included the Swiss author, poet, and bookseller Hans Werthmüller (1912–2005), the Swiss author and politician Erwin Jaeckle (1909–1997), the Swiss author, Iranologist and drug researcher Rudolf Gelpke (1928–1972), and the German publisher and author Ernst Klett (1911–1998).

Werthmüller worked in a bookshop in Basel where Gelpke and Hofmann often met. It was via Werthmüller that Hofmann contacted Ernst Jünger through the intermediary of Armin Mohler, when Hofmann sought Jünger out shortly after the Second World War. Werthmüller published a number of poetry collections and a philosophical work *Der Weltprozess und die Farben: Grundriss eines integralen Analogiesystems* (1950).[106] This book concerned a system of analogies through colours between cosmic and historical processes about which he communicated with Jünger, who was very much engaged by an understanding of history through the symbolism of colours and astrology.

Klett was a publisher of works not only by members of the Hofmann circle such as Jünger, Gelpke, Werthmüller and Jaeckel, but also non-conformist right-wing intellectuals in the post-war period, such as Julius Evola and Carl Schmitt. Klett also published the journal of culture and religion *Antaios*, which was officially edited by Mircea Eliade and Jünger (in fact they only gave their names for the project and Philipp Wolff-Windegg, the nephew of Klett, did all the editing work) and in which Gelpke published an account of his LSD experiences.[107]

Jaeckle was also a friend of Jünger but politically liberal, and wrote on drugs, poetry and natural philosophy, being concerned with human loss of contact with the elementary spirit of Nature. Jaeckle also wrote *Schicksalsrune in Orakel, Traum und Trance* (The Rune of Fate in Oracle, Dream and Trance) a book that shows how a certain situation in Jaeckle's life is reflected in a dream, a sign of the *I Ching*, in an LSD session with Gelpke taking the minutes, and two books on Paracelsus, who had taught at Basel University.

Gelpke was a scholar in the field of Islamic studies influenced by Ludwig Klages and René Guenon. He lived in Iran between 1958 and 1960, where he worked as a translator and freelance writer, studying the Iranian use of opium and hashish. Later, he taught at the University of California in 1962/3, and converted to Islam in 1967, dying in 1970. His book *Vom Rausch im Orient und Okzident* (1966) was an important study of the sophisticated literary drug culture in Iran around the use of opium and hashish, which he compared unfavourably with Western drug culture.[108] Gelpke later became critical of the role model of the isolated explorer of inner spaces, whose protocols he saw as merely legitimisations of what is considered to consist of immoral pleasures, which Western society forgives as long they are framed as research. Such protocols were like trip reports compared to the Iranian socialisation of the use of opium and hashish, which integrated inebriation into higher forms of social life manifesting in literature and the arts.

Baier considers Jünger's science fiction novel *Heliopolis* (1949), in which Jünger proposes that the leadership of a sacred monarch might in the future solve the conflicts of the world, to be a key document in understanding the perspective of Hofmann's Occultic Network on the potential of psychedelic drugs.

In *Heliopolis* a character named Antonio Peri is a prototype of the Psychonaut, a bookbinder leading an inconspicuous life who, in his spare time, uses drugs to access the hidden chambers and caves of the world. He is collector of books, whose library contains chemical and pharmacological reports of the 19th and 20th century; books concerning magic, witchcraft and demonology, the herbs and powders of sorcerers and witches; and the fiction of De Quincey, Poe, Baudelaire and ETA Hoffmann, who were all favoured by the Symbolists and Decadents of the *fin-de-siècle*. Peri thinks that each drug or combination of drugs contains a formula which gives access to a special mystery of the universe. He believes that there is a hierarchy of drugs, and that the highest formula, like the philosopher's stone, gives access to the universal mystery. However, that elixir would bring the adept to the point of death and the highest secret lies only beyond that point. That highest elixir, revealed to Peri by an adept, is a synthesis of hemp and laurel, explained in alchemical terms. Peri is an isolated non-conformist and according to Jünger, in our time drugs provide an option to lead one's life in a state of magical transformation through inebriation, which leads to immense free spaces beyond the reach of tyranny; and that this is a space to enjoy, whether alone or with a few good friends. Peri, like Gelpke and other members of Hofmann's Occultic Network, keeps protocols of his experiences and likens his experiences to astronautical journeys of inner space, which are as dangerous as journeys in physical space.

All the members of Hofmann's Occultic Network lived in the environs of Basel or within easy reach, enabling them to meet regularly. There were two active periods of experimentation with psychoactive drugs in groups, pairs or individually. The first 1949–1951 was with LSD and mescaline and a second between 1960–70, when psilocybin was added to their armoury. Baier describes Hofmann as the *primus inter pares*,[109] informally recognised as the senior member of the group. Hofmann's circle attempted to frame the operations of their collective drug culture as 'experiments', 'attempts', 'symposia' or 'séances', the best possible results being framed by Jünger as an 'initiation'. Although they did not expect every meeting to result in initiation as such, they still ritualised them by restricting numbers, adopting exotic or oriental dress, playing classical music, and celebrating the return to reality with a fine meal and wine.

Trials of LSD, in which Hofmann was himself a participant, began at Sandoz soon after the discovery of its psychoactive effects. However, Hofmann found the clinical setting and formal test procedures were not conducive to a productive psychedelic experience, so he determined to conduct his own experiments in a more sympathetic setting.[110] Hofmann had first written to Jünger in 1947 on the basis of insights that he found in *Das Abenteuerliche Herz*, sensing he might assist him in exploring the deeper meanings of the LSD experience, and he contacted him via the poet and bookseller Werthmüller and Mohler, the historian of the Conservative Revolution. In 1949 Jünger, at Hofmann's invitation, joined Hofmann, together with Mohler and Mohler's future wife, on a motoring holiday.[111] Jünger was later invited to participate in a mescaline session at the home of the publisher Ernst Klett under the supervision of the psychiatrist and psychotherapist Walter Frederking.[112]

It was through these kinds of associations that this elitist group of writers, theologians and scientists formed their own culture of inebriation. A psychonautic freemasonry of Hofmann's inner circle of friends and associates, which conducted itself according to its own rituals and observances, one which had little in common with those psychedelic cultures that later evolved in the USA and England. This group considered themselves as countercultural, but in the conservative traditionalist sense that they were in revolt against what they considered the nihilism of the modern world from which the gods had absented themselves. They considered that psychedelics might herald the dawn of a new astrological era in which the old gods would return.[113]

A History fraught with Ambiguities

Truth is always stranger than fiction, and the dual myths of the discovery of LSD as a colourful fantasy divorced from historical circumstances, or LSD as the purposeful creation of a secret society, both fade against the real-life devotion of Stoll to the works of Hermann Hesse and the activities of Hofmann's Occultic Network. Neither the difficult histories of Sandoz's wartime operations or its poor treatment of Willstätter during the Nazi era, nor Hofmann's close association with figures from the Conservative Revolution, such as Jünger or Schmitt, necessarily reflect directly on the contemporary significance of LSD. In any event they are hardly known to most afficionados of the drug. They do not necessarily affect the meaning or significance of LSD itself, which after all is just a chemical compound, its meaning something that we project onto it. However, these histories do point to a wider cultural context for the 'discovery' of the mind-altering properties of LSD, beyond the colourful psychedelic celebration that is Bicycle Day, and divorce it from the assumption that the psychedelic experience necessarily leads to liberal values.

The popular image of Hofmann's hallucinatory bicycle journey home from Sandoz depicted on souvenir mugs or badges is an icon that does not reflect the broader historical circumstances of the discovery of the psychoactive powers of LSD. It is a fantasy image born of a psychedelic culture that did not emerge until almost twenty years after Hofmann's initial discovery, a charm whose glamour isolates the discovery from the historical circumstances in which Hofmann's discovery actually took place. The real cultural history places the discovery of LSD in a historical trajectory which includes other important figures from the history of phytopharmaceutical research, other than Stoll and Hofmann. Namely, Adolf von Baeyer, Alfred Einhorn and Richard Willstätter, who as it happens were all Jewish, and two of whom were Nobel Prize winners.[114] It must also include the wartime operations of Sandoz AG and other Swiss chemical companies which allowed themselves to be compromised by the exigencies of operating during a wartime economy. When measured against the destruction of the Warsaw Ghetto and the liquidation of those confined there by the Nazis, Bicycle Day seems a meagre bookmark in the history of the 20th century. Though LSD eventually gained a worldwide reputation and became a worthy catalyst of every aspect of the arts, of spiritual practices, philosophy and sciences of the mind, its discovery should be contextualised against greater historical circumstances.

Until the genie escaped from the bottle and the popular culture of recreational use of LSD emerged in the 1960s, for medicine LSD was an experimental therapeutic of uncertain value, for intelligence services a possible truth drug, and for Hofmann and his friends it was a *phantasticum*[115] to be shared only amongst an inner circle of adepts. While celebrating Bicycle Day, devotees of LSD might do well to remember that, on the very same day, the resistance groups of the Warsaw Ghetto and their fellow captives struck for freedom in the knowledge that they would almost certainly die in the attempt.

Notes

1   To be clear, Bicycle Day is not the date on which the hallucinatory properties of LSD were first discovered through an accidental laboratory intoxication, which according to Hofmann's account occurred three days earlier on 16 April 1943.

2   See https://www.academia.edu/36538672/Why_Is_Bicycle_Day_April_19th_doc

3   The equivalent English street suffix for the use of 'rain' in German is probably 'end' or 'side'.

4   Gustacker is an historical area in Bottmingen.

5   Albert Hofmann 11.1.1906 – 29.4.2008: Schweizer Chemiker und Endecker des LSD. Lebte und forschte von 1941 bis 1968 in Bottmingen auf dem Gustacker (Oberwillerstraus 41), wo er in Rahmen eines Selbst versuchs die halluzinogene Wirkung von LSD entdeckte. Photo Credit is Sandra Lang.

6   See https://www.bikemap.net/en/r/5389566/#11.27/47.5431/7.5792

7   See https://www.alexgrey.com/art/paintings/soul/alex_grey_st_albert-2

8   See https://www.alexgrey.com/art/paintings/soul/alex-grey-new-eleusis_web

9   Wasson, Ruck, Hofmann 1978. Hofmann contributed Chapter III, 'Solving the Eleusinian Mystery', and an Afterword.

10   See for example the 'Where to celebrate Bicycle Day' listing for 2020 at https://alanaldous.com/bicycle-day-2020/

11   I had largely completed this paper when I ordered Brian Blomerth's graphic novel 'Bicycle Day' (2019), in which Dennis McKenna's introduction makes a brief reference along the lines of my initial observation that the dates of Bicycle Day and the Warsaw Ghetto Uprising coincide. I believe that my paper makes an effective development of McKenna's thoughtful notice.

12   See http://100photos.time.com/photos/jewish-boy-surrenders-warsaw

13   Also, in the *Time* collection as 'The Terror of War' http://100photos.time.com/photos/nick-ut-terror-war

14   See https://amp.theguardian.com/world/2020/sep/16/holocaust-us-adults-study

15   Milward 1979: 122–124

16   The others were J. R. Geigy AG (Geigy), Gesellschaft für Chemische Industrie in Basel AG (Ciba), F. Hoffmann-La Roche & Co. AG (Roche) and Chemische Fabrik (Straumann, Wildmann 2001)

17   The Bergier commission in Bern, also known as the ICE (Independent Commission of Experts), was formed by the Swiss government on 12 December 1996. It was an historical and legal investigation into the fate of assets which reached Switzerland as a result of the National-Socialist Regime. The final report in twenty-five volumes was published 22 March 2002 and is available at https://www.uek.ch/en/

18   Moriarty, David M (1993) *A Psychological Study of Adolf Hitler*. W.H. Green. See Appendix: 'The Medicines: Preparations Administered by Morell to Hitler during 1941–1945'

19   Atbin Djamshidian, Sabine Bernschneider-Reif, Werner Poewe, Andrew J Lees. *Banisteriopsis caapi*, a Forgotten Potential Therapy for Parkinson's Disease? Mov Disord Clin Pract. 2015 Oct 6;3(1):19-26. doi: 10.1002/mdc3.12242: https://onlinelibrary.wiley.com/doi/full/10.1002/mdc3.12242

20   The relevant exchange of letters between Willstätter and Sandoz is available through the Dodis Research Center (dodis.ch). The most significant being https://dodis.ch/18562, whose description reads 'Richard Willstätter schreibt, dass sein Rücktritt als Aufsichtsratsvorsitzender der Nürberger (sic) Sandoz AG nicht freiwillg erfolgt sei, sondern politisch bedingt war', (Richard Willstätter writes that his resignation as Chairman of the Supervisory Board of Nuremberg Sandoz AG was not voluntary but was due to politics).

21   *Switzerland, National Socialism and the Second World War. Final Report of the Independent Commission of Experts*. Section: 'Swiss subsidiaries within Nazi-controlled territory': 328. See: https://plone.unige.ch/art-adr/cases-affaires/nahschule-2013-max-silberberg-heirs-and-bundner-kunstmuseum-chur/final-report-of-the-independent-commission-of-experts-switzerland-second-world-war-2002/view

22   See http://archiv.onlinereports.ch/2001/ChemieDrittesReich.htm

23   Report of the Independent Commission of Experts, Vol.7 *Swiss Chemical Enterprises in the Third Reich*: https://www.uek.ch/en/

24   Ciba, Sandoz, and Geigy were invited to join the German Cartel

IG Farben, but instead they formed their own cartel, Basel AG in 1918. In 1929 Basel AG did join with IG Farben to create the Dual Cartel. French dyemakers then joined forming the Tripartite Cartel. When joined by the British cartel Imperial Chemical Industries in 1932, the group became the Quadripartite Cartel, which existed until 1939, when World War II forced its dissolution. See https://company-histories.com/Novartis-AG-Company-History.html

25   Sandoz 1961: 31

26   See https://prabook.com/web/arthur.stoll/2601807

27   L. 'birthing powder'.

28   Sandoz 1961: 32

29   Schnarrenberger 1987: 120

30   Stoll was himself nominated for a Nobel Prize in 1952 and again in 1953. On both occasions he was nominated by Swiss chemist Paul Hermann Müller of Geigy.

31   Schnarrenberger 1987

32   Foley 1982: 57

33   Stoll 1937

34   Schnarrenberger 1987: 113

35   Hofmann 2019: 10

36   Hofmann 1978: 3

37   Willstätter 1965: 363

38   Wiesen 2000: Passim

39   '(Willstätter) was given facilities for work in his old department in a private laboratory, called after him the "Willstätter Laboratory", and there he continued, with assistance, his research on enzymes. He seldom, however, visited this laboratory but directed the work mostly from his home in the Möhlstrasse.' (Nolan 1942)

40   Willstätter 1965: 38. Willstätter received his early education at the Realgymnasium, Nürnberg.

41   Dippel 1996: 250–251

42   Arthur Stoll, The Impact of Studies of Natural Products on

Chemical Industry in Australian Academy of Science. (1961) *The Chemistry of Natural Products: Special lectures presented at the International Symposium on the Chemistry of Natural Products*. London: Butterworths & Co Ltd.

43   Leake 1976: 136

44   Fischer 1961

45   International Archives of Allergy and Immunology, Vol. 41, No. 2-3, 1971, 475. Retrieved from https://www.karger.com/Article/ Pdf/230541

46   www.lostart.de/Content/051_ProvenienzRaubkunst/DE/ Sammler/L/Levi%20de%20Benzion,%20Mo%C3%AFse.html

47   www.secret-bases.co.uk/wiki/Mo%C3%AFse_L%C3%A9vy_ de_Benzion

48   Harclerode, Pittaway, 1999: 141

49   Raeber was a prominent art dealer, vice president of the Swiss syndicate of art dealers and its most active member. He was involved in various looted art transactions and possessed certain paintings on the Allied List of looted art. https://www.lootedart. com/MVI3RM469661

50   Yeide 2009: 456

51   Following a number of further changes of hands, in 1999 the painting was acquired by the Birmingham Museum of Art in Alabama. Richard Howard, the founding director of the Birmingham Museum of Art, had been one of the 'Monuments Men' depicted in the 2014 film of the same name, directed by George Clooney. See: https://www.artsbma.org/collection/ entree-dun-gave-source-of-a-mountain-stream/

52   Hermann Hesse, Dedication to Arthur Stoll on his 70th Birthday in Festschrift Herrn Prof. Dr. Arthur Stoll zum 70. Geburtstag, 8. Januar 1957. (Festschrift for Prof. Dr. Arthur Stoll on his 70th birthday, January 8, 1957 Arbeiten aus dem Gebiet der Naturstoffchemie. Basel: Birkhäuser 1957. This translation taken from Royal Society Obituary for Arthur Stoll: Leopold Ruzicka. 1972, Arthur Stoll, 1887–1971 Biogr. Mems Fell. R. Soc.18, 566–593

53   Swiss Literary Archives (SLA), Hallwylstrasse 15, CH-3003 Bern. At https://ead.nb.admin.ch/html/hesse.html

54   Bran 1982: 17

55   Stoll 1997: 65

56   An odourless garlic extract

57   Stoll, 1997: 65–67

58   Ibid.

59   Weaver 1977: 117

60   Ibid.

61   Sirotkina 2019: Ch. 5 'By the Fourth Way'.

62   Translated as *LSD: My Problem Child*. First English edition is
      Hofmann (1980)

63   Nichols 2003

64   'In 1938, I produced the twenty-fifth substance in this series of
      lysergic acid derivatives: lysergic acid diethylamide, abbreviated
      LSD-25.' Hofmann 1980

65   Hofmann 2019: 3–4

66   Nichols 2003

67   Drug doses are normally measured in milligrams, not micrograms
      which are one hundredth of a milligram.

68   Jay 2018

69   Hofmann 2019: 21

70   Jay 2018

71   Interview in Fry, P., Long, M. (1977). Beyond the Mechanical
      Mind: an investigation by Peter Fry and Malcolm Long based
      on the ABC radio series 'And Something Else is Happening',
      Australian Broadcasting Commission.

72   Kleiner 2008: 157–172

73   Fry and Long, 1977

74   Fry & Long 1977: 102

75   A useful account of Willis Harman's career can be found in
      Kleiner (2008). Harman authored numerous books linking the
      ideas of the human potential movement to enlightened business
      and economic practices as well as titles of New Age philosophy
      and on parapsychology.

76   Harman was definitely in error when he claimed in the broadcast
      that 'by 1938 they had synthesized psilocybin, LSD and about

thirty other drugs.' It was only in 1957 that French mycologist Roger Heim accompanied R Gordon Wasson on one of his Mexican expeditions and was able to identify the psychoactive mushrooms Wasson was investigating as Psilocybe species. After cultivating the mushrooms in France, Heim sent samples for analysis to Albert Hofmann who isolated and identified the psychoactive compounds in *Psilocybe Mexicana* and was later able to synthesise them. The first chemical study of *P. mexicana* was made by Hofmann in 1958, who isolated psilocybin in crystalline form (Guzmán 1983). However, it seems likely that Harman's assertions were a confused account of information circulating in the US West Coast elite psychedelic community.

77   Milek 1980: 181; Weaver 1977: Ch 7 '…and about drugs'

78   Leary, Metzner, 1963: 167–182

79   See for example Stafford P. (1983). *Psychedelics Encyclopedia.* Boston, MA: Houghton Mifflin.

80   Horowitz 1976: Accessed at Accessed at: https://erowid.org/culture/characters/hofmann_albert/hofmann_albert_interview1.shtml

81   Leary 1982: 315

82   Various versions of Stahlman's claims heave been posted online. The most complete account, edited by a follower of his claims, can be found at: https://ionamillersubjects.weebly.com/lsd-althistory.html

83   Surette 1994: 48

84   Surette 1994: 5

85   Günter Engel and Rudolf Giger, 'Dr Albert Hofmann's work on ergot alkaloids and its influence on the development of pharmaceuticals at Sandoz', in Engel and Hofmann (2006)

86   Sandoz 1961: 39

87   Hofmann 2019: 6

88   Ziolkowski 2013: 149–157

89   See: Ziolkowski 1974; Ziolkowski 2013; Abbott 1991

90   Baigent, Leigh, Lincoln 1982: See Ch. 6 'The Grand Masters and the Underground Stream'

91   Timothy Leary's 'League for Spiritual Discovery', the third incarnation of Leary's efforts to promote LSD, was preceded

by the International Federation for Internal Freedom and the Castalia Foundation, named after the hierarchical spiritual Castalian Order in Hesse's novel *The Glass Bead Game*.

92   Jünger 1929/1939

93   English edition: Jünger, E (Auth), Berman, R A (Ed), Friese, T (Trans). (2012) *The Adventurous Heart: Figures and Capriccios.* Candor, NY: Telos Press Publication

94   Hofmann 2019: 110

95   Jünger 2012: 55

96   Ibid. 59

97   Ibid. 54

98   Ibid. 63

99   Hofmann 2019: 110

100   Hofmann 2019: 110

101   Jünger 2012: 178

102   Ibid. 37

103   Ibid. 34

104   Karl Baier "Early Psychonauts: Albert Hoffmann's Occultic Network". See: https://www.amsterdamhermetica.nl/esswe-2-4-july-2019

105   Baier 2019

106   'The World Process and Colours: An outline of an integral analogical system'.

107   Rudolf Gelpke, Von Fahrten in den Weltraum der Seele (Albert Hofmann gewidmet) [Journey to the Outer Space of the Soul (dedicated to Albert Hofmann)]. In Eliade, M and Jünger, E, Antaios. Band III, No. 5, January 1962.

108   'On intoxication in the Orient and Occident'

109   'First among equals'

110   Baier 2019

111   Hofmann 1995

112   Ibid.

113   Baier notes that as well as conservative revolutionary political

thinkers such as Jünger and Carl Schmitt, Klett published traditionalist occultist Julius Evola's *Metaphysik des Sexus* (1962). Evola in his *Rivolta contro il mondo moderno* (1934) follows the Hindu doctrine of Yugas (world ages) of which he considers the world to be in the fourth and worst, the Kali Yuga, a dark age of conflict and spiritual degeneration.

114 Adolf von Baeyer, Nobel Prize in Chemistry 1905. Richard Willstätter, Nobel Prize in Chemistry 1915, for his research on plant pigments, especially chlorophyll, in which Arthur Stoll assisted.

115 This was the drug classification in the system devised by German pharmacologist Louis Lewin (1850–1929) in which he included Peyote. It was used for LSD in the report by Werner Stoll, Arthur Stoll's son, a psychiatrist in the first systematic trial of LSD. The trial included multiple doses given to schizophrenic individuals, who could hardly have consented. See Stoll, W A. Lysergsäure-Diäthylamid, ein Phantastikum aus der Mutterkorngruppe. [Lysergic Acid Diethylamide, a Phantasticant of the Ergot Class.] Schweizer Archiv für Neurologie und Psychiatrie. 1947. 60 279–323

6

Revisiting Jünger's *Godenholm*
A Story of Psychedelic Initiation

Albert Hofmann and Ernst Jünger's *Visit to Godenholm*

Ernst Jünger's short novel *Visit to Godenholm* (*VTG*), [1] first published in Germany in 1952 as *Besuch auf Godenholm,* is now available in English language translation for the first time, thanks to the efforts of its translator Annabel Moynihan, and Edda Publishing.[2]

It is published hardbound with dust jacket, limited to 400 copies in total: 360 standard copies and a special limited edition consisting of 40 copies. The special limited edition comes in a boxed set with a hand-made linoleum print, signed and numbered by the book's illustrator Fredrik Söderberg. Publication as a limited fine edition indicates the esteem in which the author Ernst Jünger is held by the publisher. Other than in the relevant volume of the collected works of Jünger's considerable literary output, *Besuch auf Godenholm* has rarely been republished in Germany since its appearance in 1952, a testament to its obscure and esoteric nature.

As part of the cultural history of psychedelics, *VTG* is important if only because it contains what is probably the first account of the LSD experience in what is ostensibly a work of fiction. More significantly, at this early stage in the history of LSD, it places its use in the context of an esoteric gnosis reserved for the few. Although set in Norway, it is made clear that the context is Germany in the wake of the Second World War, when it was still a country occupied under partition by the Americans, British, French and Russians.[3]

The novel makes no direct reference to a drug-induced experience, but the hallucinatory sequence at the heart of the book is derived from Jünger's experiences with LSD,[4] as attested by Albert Hofmann himself. *Besuch auf Godenholm* was published two years after Jünger first met the chemist and in the year after their first shared LSD experience, which took place in 1951. According to Hofmann:

> About the same time that Aldous Huxley carried out his experiments with mescaline, I held LSD sessions with the well-known German author Ernst Jünger in order to gain a more profound knowledge of the visionary experiences produced by the drug in the human mind. Ernst Jünger recorded his experiences in an essay entitled *Besuch auf Godenholm* (Vittorio Klosterman, Frankfurt a. M. 1952), which gives in literary form the essence of his interpretations.[5]

Hofmann later described how Jünger incorporated into *VTG* a specific event from a shared LSD session of early February 1951. The trip took place in the living room of the Hofmanns' house in Bottmingen in Switzerland, in the company of Heribert Konzett (1912–2004), an Austrian physician and pharmacologist. Hofmann invited Konzett in order to have medical aid on hand if necessary, due to Hofmann's concerns about dosing the celebrated author and sensitive creative individual, Ernst Jünger, with a powerful psychoactive drug.[6] During their trip Hofmann and Jünger 'contemplated the haze of smoke that ascended with the ease of thought from a Japanese incense stick.' According to Hofmann 'Jünger has assimilated the mentioned spectacle of the incense stick into literature, in his story *Besuch auf Godenholm*, in which deeper experiences of drug inebriation also play a part' and Hofmann then excerpts the relevant descriptive paragraph from Jünger's short novel.[7]

Jünger's novella *Besuch auf Godenholm* preceded Aldous Huxley's first published account of his mescaline experiences in *The Doors of Perception* (1954) by two years. Huxley's essay concentrated on the aesthetics of the mescaline experience, the mechanics of perception and a somewhat rarefied conception of its spiritual potential. By way of contrast, Jünger's novella takes place in the context of an esoteric initiation under the guidance of a magus named Schwarzenberg, a figure who appears in a number of Jünger's works under the name Magister, Schwarzenberg, or Nigromontanus. Both of the latter mean Black Mountain, an appropriate name for the *eminence grise* depicted in Jünger's book *Das abenteuerliche Herz* (1929), recently republished as *The Adventurous Heart* (2012). It describes how 'Among the things Nigromontanus taught me was the certain existence among us of a select group of men who have long withdrawn from the libraries, and from the dust of the public arena, who are at work in the innermost spaces, in the obscurest of Tibets.'[8] Jünger's *The Adventurous Heart* reveals a disposition towards the Left Hand Path, while Huxley's inclinations are clearly contrary.

The magus figure appears in other of Jünger's works, including the novella *Heliopolis* (1949), which is also drug-themed and includes a cryptic reference to Albert Hofmann. The library of the central character, Antonio Peri, a psychoactive drug adventurer, contains 'a heavy old volume by the Heidelberg psychologists on the extract of mescal buttons, and a paper on the phantastica of ergot by Hofmann-Bottmingen.'[9] Hofmann's place of residence at that time was the Swiss town of Bottmingen on the outskirts of Basel. Researchers have principally identified the fictional figure of Schwarzenberg/Nigromontanus with the German philosopher Hugo Fischer (1897–1975), with whom Jünger had travelled to Norway in 1935. Jünger recounted that journey in *'Myrdun' Briefe aus Norwegen* (1943),[10] in which Fischer is identified only under the title Magister. Fischer later emigrated from Germany to Norway in 1938[11] and Schwarzenberg is credited with the same pre-war relocation in *Godenholm*, though he is almost certainly a composite figure used by Jünger to represent a custodian and teacher of esoteric knowledge.[12] In *Besuch auf Godenholm* (1952) Jünger almost certainly intentionally identifies Schwarzenberg with the controversial spiritual teacher George Ivanovich Gurdjieff (1872–1949), whom Jünger mentions by name in *Der Waldgang* (1951). The account of Schwarzenberg's travels in *Besuch auf Godenholm* closely resemble Gurdjieff's early expeditions to Central Asia, his presence in Russia during the Kerensky Government (1917), and his later presence in Berlin (1921–22).[13] Jünger referred to Gurdjieff in connection with magical drugs in his letter to Hofmann of December 1961.[14]

In *Besuch auf Godenholm* Schwarzenberg embraces a science of catastrophe in which 'all discoveries were preceded by periods of conflagration.' Given the post-war situation in Germany, Moltner, the protagonist in *VTG*, lives with a sense of catastrophe, and senses that 'the shipwreck had already happened and he was floating on the ruins... Security had vanished, values became provisional; yet ancestral inheritance remained.'[15] Salvation might lay in the work of initiatic groups behind the scenes to usher in change, as guided by Schwarzenberg.

> The plan to assess the situation in small groups – and test their limits in experiments was not so senseless. There was nothing new about this idea; there had always been such a plan during great transitions – in deserts, cloisters, in hermitages, in stoic and gnostic communities, in circles surrounding philosophers, prophets and initiates.[16]

Jünger expressed the same view in a letter to Hofmann.

> Wine has already changed much, has brought new gods and
> a new humanity with it. But wine is to the new substances as
> classical physics is to modern physics. These things should
> only be tried in small circles. I cannot agree with the thoughts
> of Huxley, that possibilities for transcendence could here be
> given to the masses. Indeed, this does not involve comforting
> fictions, but rather realities, if we take the matter earnestly. And
> few contacts will suffice here for the setting of courses and
> guidance. It also transcends theology and belongs in the chapter
> of theogony[17], as it necessarily entails entry into a new house, in
> the astrological sense.[18]

Jünger's belief in cycles of destruction and renewal is clearly
influenced by his experience of two world wars but is also clearly occult
in nature. At the same time as operating on a cosmic or national scale,
these cycles are reflected in his commitment to the character-forming
nature of extreme experiences such as combat in war, which as we shall
see he extends to the psychological rigours of psychedelic experience.

The Godenholm Story

The story opens with its protagonist Moltner standing on a beach
musing, then swiftly moves on to a description of two men, Einar
and Moltner, and one woman, Ulma, being rowed on a foggy winter's
day from the Norwegian coastal town of Sandnes to an imaginary
island named Godenholm.[19] They are on their way to a meeting with
Schwarzenberg, the magus figure under whose tutelage they have been
receiving an esoteric education since the summer. The narrative centres
on third person descriptions of the experiences, thoughts and emotions
of Moltner and Einar.

The character Einar, depicted as a veteran of the First World War
who fought in the trenches, is clearly based on Jünger himself. However,

the story centres on Einar's friend Moltner, a physician and neurologist who served in the war as a medic, culminating with him experiencing a cathartic psychedelic epiphany. Moltner, a critical intellectual with dark curly hair, a spiritual gadfly drawn from one spiritual teacher to another, is continually contrasted with the pragmatic blond Einar who is of peasant Flemish stock. Moltner is described as sanguine, optimistic and cheerful, while Einar is phlegmatic, unemotional and stolidly calm. Moltner is a neurologist, while Einar is a prehistorian who has studied the megalithic monuments of Europe, which is how he encountered the magus Schwarzenberg.

The outlook on the fogbound island of Godenholm is gloomy and in translation the word 'grey' occurs four times in the first two pages of the story and regularly thereafter. The weather is frequently referred to as affecting the mental state of the characters. *VTG* is filled with a sense of elemental powers and their interaction with every aspect of life, and Jünger refers to the 'three natural realms' of Air, Fire and Water as the system by which Schwarzenberg arranges his collection of natural curiosities. Just as the dominant colour in *VTG* is grey, the dominant element in the novella is water. Fish abound in the story as the element's native inhabitants in the waters around the island of Godenholm, creatures whose behaviour is linked to the phases of the moon. In the heart of the psychedelic phase of the story, Moltner is drawn into a turbulent underwater realm before emerging into a realm of golden light.

The Norwegian landscape is depicted as monochrome and fogbound, and the book's illustrations by Frederick Söderberg are likewise largely monochrome. The description of the countryside around Sandnes is that of an idealised rural past, unchanged since the Middle Ages. It is implied by shared regional dress that both Einar and Ulma (whose father is a local farmer) are connected with the local region where 'the earth was spiritualized and made cerebral by the long nights.'[20] Einar and Ulma are at ease with Schwarzenberg's rough and ready retainers, his factotum Gaspar and housekeeper Erdmuthe, who are imbued with primaeval energies, while Moltner finds their presence unsettling.

Einar, Moltner and Ulma have enjoyed an idyllic Norwegian summer of naked swimming and beach picnics, while having regular sessions with their teacher Schwarzenberg. Their psychedelic experience takes place during the winter solstice, when the sun barely peeks over the horizon in northern latitudes. The winter solstice is Yule in the Nordic pagan calendar, a time of transition, and frequent references are made to other aspects of Nordic mythology, such as the presence of the goddesses Freya and Herta.

In a familiar pattern in the guru-disciple relationship, the story describes a honeymoon period for Moltner in which feelings of guilt and pain melt away in the guru's presence, and nothing warns that severe tests will follow. As the narrative progresses, Moltner feels neglected by his guru Schwarzenberg, who seems careless, and disinterested in his health and mental state. He develops paranoid thoughts about Schwarzenberg's intentions towards him in the very moments leading up to his psychedelic epiphany. Immediately prior to their shared psychedelic experience even Einar and Ulma are feeling uneasy. Moltner confronts Schwarzenberg with his doubts and his intention to leave there and then, but in the midst of the argument he slips into a psychedelic reverie.

As indicated earlier, it is not made explicit in *VTG* that the psychedelic experiences of Schwarzenberg's students are drug induced. They apparently occur spontaneously in his presence, in the same way that the mere presence of certain Sufi masters or a short benediction by one can induce an altered state of consciousness. Regardless, we shall see, the description of the experiences of Einar, Moltner and Ulma under the influence of Schwarzenberg follow the pattern of a guided psychedelic experience.

The Godenholm Trip

Visit to Godenholm has fourteen brief chapters, the last seven of which are dedicated to the psychedelic sequence. It is thus evenly balanced between the setting of the scene and introduction to the characters, and the psychedelic experiences of Moltner, Einar and Ulma. Jünger's description of the psychedelic experiences of the characters is convincing, evidence of both his own drug adventures and his considerable experience as an author. In common with Hofmann's descriptions of his own shared LSD sessions, Schwarzenberg pays attention to set and setting. The room has been elaborately prepared by Schwarzenberg for their trip, with seats arranged for the participants in a dimly lit room: 'Sigrid had brought the tea. The samovar stood on the mantelpiece; the cups had been set next to the candelabra. The fire glowed in quiet splendour.'[21]

Effects typical of LSD are described, with time tremendously extended, super-acuity of visual perception, auditory and visual hallucinations, and the imaginative interpretation of everyday sights and sounds. The housekeeping activities of Gaspar and servant Sigrid outside are interpreted as sinister troll-like scrapings and scratchings. The howl of the yard dog is interpreted as that of the monstrous wolf *Fenrir* of the *Edda*.[22] *Fenrir* is an important figure in the events of *Ragnarök*, the apocalypse of Nordic myth in which, after a destructive battle of the gods, the world is born anew, destruction and renewal being a repeated theme within the *Godenholm* story. The descriptions of the participants' trips are laced with references to figures from Nordic mythology. Moltner hears the song of the *Erlking*, an invitation to enter the other world, the realm of the dead from which one may never return. The *Erlking* is a figure synonymous with King Herla, or Odin as leader of the wild hunt, a ghostly group of hunters on horseback with hounds galloping across the night sky, a portent of catastrophe. Anyone who sees them may be carried away to the land of the dead. Moltner, Einar and Ulma all experience an awareness of the inevitability of death and decay.

The trip takes place by stages, as if conducted from one otherworldly domain to another. Moments of intense psychic pain precede moments of equally intense sensory pleasure, with the whole process guided by the magus Schwarzenberg. The faces of the participants become painfully revelatory, disclosing their inner nature and emotional states. Schwarzenberg repeatedly and intrusively addresses Moltner with the question 'Isn't it true, don't you know yet more?' each time mercilessly pushing Moltner further and further within himself. The phrase is an echo of his insistence to Moltner at the outset: 'you know that you are suffering – thus you know more. That is the artesian point.'[23] This reflects Jünger's belief in the personally illuminating nature of pain and the ability to endure it. Moltner experiences this questioning by Schwarzenberg 'like a blow from a weapon whose existence he didn't know about. It was comparable to the kind of shock one experiences from an attack that is simultaneously violent and obscene.'[24] Eventually Moltner feels stripped to the bone, exhausted and thrown into a psychic encounter for which he is simply unprepared. The experience of a severe initiatic process, to which the participant is not equal and fails, is also a recurrent theme of Jünger's book *The Adventurous Heart* (2012).

The trip proceeds with a sense of musical rhythm, conducted by the sounds of the nearby ocean and a storm, thundering outside the room in which the participants are seated. As the sounds diminish in intensity so does the trip and Moltner feels a shared complicity in communing with something entirely 'other' than the people actually present. As the intensity diminishes, 'All sounds were now hushed. The ancient serpent began to move off silently'[25] — the serpent being a symbol for Jünger of the dangerous wisdom of heretical gnosis.[26] The participants' painful sense of personal exposure is replaced by the experience of typical geometric and naturalistic visualisations, and this is the point at which the moment of the spiral of incense smoke related by Hofmann is included in the narration of the trip. After a last plunge by Moltner into a watery vortex filled with marine life, the sudden unexpected intrusion into the room by Erdmuthe the housekeeper, Gaspar the factotum, and the yard dog, signals a return to the world of normality. Moltner emerges into a domain of golden light with a sense of recovery and renewal. For a moment, to his horror, it appears that Schwarzenberg intends to again intensify matters but he relents, saying to Moltner, 'You are right – we shouldn't go any further.'[27]

Two chapters are largely dedicated to Einar's own psychedelic experiences. The contrast between Einar and Moltner is reiterated, as in Einar's earthiness and Moltner's intellectuality. Einar steps into a 'not unfamiliar landscape' and doesn't descend so deeply as Moltner. Einar is clearly based on Jünger himself, not only by means of references to his First World War experiences, but also his philosophical views. In particular by reference to Einar's description as being one who 'loved pain as the ultimate mark of reality',[28] a view expressed in Jünger's essay *Über den Schmerz* (1934); originally published just after the Nazi seizure of power, and more recently published in translation.[29] The ability to withstand pain and to face death unflinchingly is, in Jünger's assessment, an indicator of a higher level of being and this aspect of his nature expressly defines the nature of Einar's psychedelic experience. 'The closeness of death attracted him' and he 'welcomed the risk that Moltner had avoided.'[30]

Ulma shares some of Einar's experiences of psychedelic consciousness, in which reminiscences of First World War trench warfare are mixed with the experience of being amongst ancient defensive earthworks. These earthworks, the subject of Einar's prehistorical studies, double as grave sites and mirror Jünger's experiences of trench walls built over the bodies of sacrificed comrades. Einar experiences a meeting with his deceased mother and father, which reads powerfully as if based on an experience of Jünger himself, an account which would have comfortably fitted among the dreamlike passages which make up *The Adventurous Heart*.[31]

The traumatic aspects of Ulma, Einar and Moltner's experiences finally fade into a comforting golden glow of ancient sunlight. The ancestral mother is present as Frigga, and there is awareness that they have all shared an intimation of a great mystery, outside the cycles of Time, one which is intimately connected with human mortality. The spell is broken and they are back in the room. On coming down Moltner feels reborn, he is reconciled to Gaspar and Erdmuthe, whose earthiness he had previously found alienating, and he recovers from his sense of an absence of any ability as a psychiatric doctor to really heal his patients. Sensitive to set and setting, Schwarzenberg has made prior arrangements, and servants bring in food and drink as a comforting and celebratory closure to their adventure.

Though Schwarzenberg is a stern and demanding psychopomp, Jünger's account of the LSD session is one which offers a psychotherapeutic outcome for his initiates Einar and Moltner, who are suffering from the trauma of Germany's defeat and its catastrophic aftermath, at a time when clinical investigations were at a very early stage. It presages later developments where LSD is seen as supporting psychotherapeutic intervention but sets it in a context of an esoteric initiation, underpinned by a seam of Nordic mythopoetic imagery. Jünger was an amateur scientist who studied entomology, who mixed his scientific bent with a deeply occult world view.

Godenholm in Context

To understand the book's significance at the time of its initial publication it is important to place *Visit to Godenholm* in its cultural context and its place in the long list of Jünger's other literary works. I have already mentioned that the figure of Schwarzenberg is based in part on Jünger's friend Hugo Fischer, whose travels in Norway with Jünger were recorded by him in *Myrdun* (1943). *Besuch auf Godenholm* was only the second of Jünger's fictional works to be published in Germany following the occupation by Allied forces following the end of the World War Two. In fact, Jünger was forbidden to publish between 1945 and 1949 in the occupied zones of Germany, governed by the American and British military.[32] The Allied occupation of Western Germany actually continued until 5th May 1955, a matter of considerable distress to Jünger as he makes clear in *Der Waldang* (1951). A *Liste der Auszusondernden Literatur* (List of Proscribed Literature), published in the Soviet Zone, was used by The Information Control Division of the American Military Government in Germany. The list identified books that were to be destroyed, their publication and sale forbidden. In Jünger's case, a number of his works were cited from the list which, due to their militaristic nature, had earlier found favour with the Nazi regime, including *In Stahlgewittern* (Storms of Steel) and *Waldchen 125* (Copse 125).[33]

Jünger's literary career commenced with, and significantly still rests on, his accounts of his experiences of trench warfare during the First World War. He was decorated twice with the *Iron Cross* and then *Pour le Mérite* known as the 'Blue Max', Prussia's highest order of merit, awarded strictly as a recognition of extraordinary personal achievement. On account of this, and his growing literary reputation, Jünger was a person of considerable standing and was widely read in Germany during the inter-war period and World War Two. The later pre-war works by Jünger focused on the increasing impact of technology on society, influenced by his experience of mechanised warfare in World War One. However, in part under the influence of his drug experiences, Jünger's works took an Expressionist or even Surrealist turn with the dreamlike sequences of *Das Abenteuerliche Herz* (1938), which alienated Jünger from the Nazi leadership.[34] They wanted to exploit his literary status by inducting him into the German Academy of Literature in November 1933, an offer which Jünger declined.[35]

Although published seven years after the end of the Second World War, Jünger makes clear references in *Der Waldgang* (1951) and *VTG* to his continued disillusionment with the war and its outcome, which he refers to in the latter as 'the catastrophe'. In *Der Waldgang*, recently published in English as *The Forest Passage* (2013), Jünger expresses his anger and resentment at the defeat of Germany in the Second World War, as well as the Allied occupation. Indeed, Jünger makes repeated references to living under occupation and the word *fragebogen* (questionnaire) appears several times,[36] as well frequent references to questions and being questioned. These are a clear reference to the questionnaire that prominent individuals from the Nazi era were required to complete as part of the denazification process, a requirement to which Jünger refused to submit. Curiously the Introduction to the recent translation of *Der Waldgang* makes no mention of Jünger's obvious and repeated references to the questionnaire, though this is critical to understanding the cultural context of both *Der Waldgang* and *VTG*. Importantly, *The Forest Passage* represented Jünger's declaration of his withdrawal from the world of politics, a retreat into a rural sanctuary from which to observe and write from a distance. In *Godenholm*, Jünger as Einar is seeking a way forward, the ability to envisage a positive outcome from the catastrophe of Germany's defeat in World War Two, which he may have found in part through his encounters with LSD.

Jünger's *Visit to Godenholm* certainly repays repeated reading, as each new visit reveals fresh nuances and further associations with other aspects of Jünger's life and works. Jünger, a major European writer, honoured with many literary and cultural awards, chronicled the 20th century from a unique perspective. Historically, psychedelic drugs have been associated with progressive politics and the radical left through the popular culture of the 1960s, which embraced LSD as an agent of change and personal liberation. Jünger's fascination with the experience of psychedelic drugs and his placing it in a ritualistic and initiatory context represents a curious convergence of psychedelics with his extreme conservatism and anti-democratic sentiments. [37] Though his fascination reflects Jünger's belief in the productive nature of extreme experience, it may also require a revision of existing assumptions and tropes concerning the social and psychological impact of the psychedelic experience.

Notes

1   Due to the small print run, the Edda edition is hard to find. The author notes a recent paperback translation of *VTG* but cannot vouch for its accuracy or quality. All references and quotations here are to the Edda edition.

2   See   https://www.carlabrahamsson.com/edda-publishing/ernst-jungers-godenholm-available-in-english/

3   There were also small Belgian, Polish and Luxembourgish zones of occupation. Although the Federal Republic was established in May 1949, the Allied occupation of Western Germany continued until 5 May 1955, when the General Treaty (German: *Deutschlandvertrag*) came into force.

4   And also, no doubt Jünger's prior experiences with mescaline. Jünger had experimented with various psychoactive drugs since his youth, including hashish and mescaline. See Loose 1974: 121

5   See Hofmann's preface in Huxley 1977: *xi*

6   Although Hofmann does not mention it, Konzett actually worked at Sandoz. Konzett studied at the Universities of Innsbruck and Vienna, where he received his doctorate in 1936. Until 1946 he worked at the Institute of Pharmacology, University of Vienna and then went to Britain. From 1946 until his appointment to Innsbruck Medical School in 1957, he conducted research at the Pharmacological Laboratory of the Sandoz Ltd., Basel. See: https://www.i-med.ac.at/pharmakologie/nachruf_konzett.html

7   Hofmann 2013: 115

8   Jünger 2012. See the section headed *Solitary Sentinels*.

9   Hofmann 2013: 114

10 *Myrdun* was first published in 1943 in occupied Norway as a field edition for the *Wehrmacht*, under the protection of the German Military Forces. See: http://www.juenger-haus.de/1921-1945,177.html

11 In 1939 Hugo Fischer moved on to England, staying one step ahead of the Nazis. Like Jünger, Fischer was one of the representatives of the conservative resistance to the liberal democracy of the Weimar Republic (1918–1933), but who later lost any sympathy with the Nazi regime and therefore was at risk of incarceration or death. It is ironic therefore that *Mydrun*

was published in Oslo as a field edition for German troops in occupied Norway, with Fischer's identity concealed with a *nom de plume*.

12   The fact that Jünger's father, an apothecary, bought a pharmacy in the town of Schwarzenberg (Hervier 1990) may be the reason for Jünger choosing this name for his magus.

13   See: http://www.gurdjieff.org/chronology.htm

14   Hofmann 2013: 120

15   Junger 2015: 19

16   Ibid.

17   That is an account of the origin and descent of the gods. Jünger clearly has an occult, myth-based theory of history.

18   Hofmann 2013: 120

19   Although the Island of Godenholm is fictional there is a town of Sandnes in Norway, situated as described in a fjord. The fjord Gandsfjorden is situated north-south and ends in the centre of Sandnes.

20   Jünger 2015: 13

21   Ibid.: 51

22   The 13th century Old Norse work of literature, which is a major source for Scandinavian mythology.

23   Jünger 2015: 53

24   Ibid. 55

25   Ibid. 65

26   Loose 1974: 65–66

27   Jünger 2015: 69

28   Jünger 2015: 70

29   Jünger 2008

30   Jünger 2015: 70

31   For Hofmann's appreciation of *The Adventurous Heart* see Chapter 7 of Hofmann's *LSD my Problem Child* (2013), 'Radiance from Ernst Jünger'.

32   Loose 1974: 16

33   Breitenkamp 1953

34   Neaman 1999: 39

35   Morat 2012: 666

36   Jünger 2014: 8, 9, 12, 17

37   A study by the author investigates this conundrum. See Piper
      2015

Bibliography

Abbott, S. (1991) *Fictions of Freemasonry: Freemasonry and the German Novel*. Detroit, MI: Wayne State University Press.

Abraham RH, McKenna, T, Sheldrake, R (1992) *Trialogues at the edge of the West: Chaos, Creativity, and the Resacralization of the World*. Santa Fe: Bear & Company

Albert, NG (2017). *Lesbian Decadence: Representations in Art and Literature of Fin-de Siècle France*. New York: NY, Harrington Park Press

Apollinaire, G (1918). *Calligrammes, poèmes de la paix et de la guerre 1913–1916*. Paris, France: Mercure de France

Baigent, M, Leigh R, and Lincoln, H (1982) *The Holy Blood and the Holy Grail*. London: Jonathan Cape

Baigent, M et al. (1982*) The Holy Blood and the Holy Grail*. London: Jonathan Cape

Barnes, SM (1995) 'The Higher Powers: Fred M. Smith and the Peyote Ceremonies' in *Dialogue: A Journal of Mormon Thought*: Vol. 28, no. 4, 91–97

Beard, M (2002). *The Invention of Jane Harrison*. Cambridge: MA, Harvard University Press

Beckstead, RT (2007) *The Restoration and The Sacred Mushroom: Did Joseph Smith Use Psychedelics to Facilitate His Visionary Experiences?* Salt Lake City, UT. Sunstone Symposium. Online: https://sunstone.org/the-restoration-and-the-sacred-mushroom-did-joseph-smith-use-psychedelics-to-facilitate-his-visionary-experiences/

Beringer, K (1927) *Der Meskalinrausch seine Geschichte und Erscheinungsweise*, Berlin: Julius Springer

Berridge, V (1988) 'The Origins of The English Drug "Scene": 1890-1930'. *Medical History*: 32: 51-64

Blomerth, B. (2019) *Brian Blomerth's Bicycle Day.* Brooklyn, NY: Anthology Editions

Bloom, H (1979) *The Flight to Lucifer: A Gnostic fantasy*. New York: Farrar, Straus, Giroux

Bloom, H (2005) *Novelists and Novels*. New York: Chelsea House

Boon, M (2006) 'Foreword' to Benjamin, W. *On Hashish*. Cambridge, MA: Harvard University Press

Boon, M (2009) *The Road of Excess: A History of Writers on Drugs*. Cambridge, MA: Harvard University Press

Breitenkamp, EC (1953) *United States Information Control Division and its effect on German publishers and writers, 1945 to 1949.* Grand Forks, ND: University Station

Butts, M (2008) *Journals of Mary Butts*. New Haven, CT: Yale University Press

Carr, VC (2004) *Dos Passos: A Life*. Evanston, Ill: Northwestern University Press

Cendrars, C (Auth), Boucharenc, M (Ed) (2006) *Panorama de la pègre*. Paris: Denoël

Clayton, A (2012) *Netherwood: Last Resort of Aleister Crowley*. London: Accumulator Press

Crowley, A (1989) *The Confessions of Aleister Crowley: An Autobiography*. London: Arkana

Damon, SF (1924) *William Blake, his Philosophy and Symbols*. Boston, MA: Houghton Mifflin

Damon, SF (2013) *A Blake Dictionary: The Ideas and Symbols of William Blake*. Hanover, N.H.: Dartmouth College Press

David C Downing (1995) *Planets in Peril: A Critical Study of CS Lewis's Ransom Trilogy*. Amherst: University of Massachusetts Press

Deichmann, U (1999) 'The Expulsion of Jewish Chemists and Biochemists from Academia in Nazi Germany' in *Perspectives on Science*. Online: DOI: 10.1162/posc.1999.7.1.1

Dery, M (2012) 'Been There, Pierced That: Apocalypse Culture and the Escalation of Subcultural Hostilities' in *I must not think Bad Thoughts*. Minneapolis, MIN: University of Minnesota Press

Dettwiler, W et al. (2014) *Novartis: How a leader in healthcare was created out of Ciba, Geigy and Sandoz*. London: Profile Books

Dippel, JVH (1996) *Bound Upon a Wheel of Fire: Why So Many German Jews Made the Tragic Decision to Remain in Nazi Germany*. New York, NY: Basic Books

Ellis, H (1902) 'Mescal: A Study of a Divine Plant' in *Popular Science Monthly*: Vol. 61

Engel, G (Editor) and Hofmann, A (Celebrated). (2006) *Exploring the Frontiers - In Celebration of Albert Hofmann's 100th birthday*. Basel: Schwabe

English, C (2022) *The Gallery of Miracles & Madness: Insanity, Art and Hitler's first Mass-Murder*. London: William Collins

Everitt, P (2016) *The Cactus and the Beast: Investigating the Role of Peyote and Mescaline in the Magick of Aleister Crowley*. MA Thesis: University of Amsterdam

Faderman, L (1992). *Odd Girls and Twilight Lovers: A History of Lesbian Life in Twentieth Century America*. New York: Penguin

Fischer, M (1961) *Sammlung Arthur Stoll. Skulpturen und Gemälde des 19. und 20. Jahrhunderts*. Zürich: Schweizerisches Institut für Kunstwissenschaft.

Foley, PB (1982) *Beans, Roots and Leaves: A History of the Chemical Therapy of Parkinsonism*. Doctoral dissertation submitted to the Bavarian Julius Maximilian University

Freedman, J (1993*) Professions of Taste: Henry James, British Aestheticism, and Commodity Culture*. Stanford, CA: Stanford University Press

Friedrich Bran, MP (1982) *Hermann Hesse und seine literarischen Zeitgenossen: 2. repoertes Hermann-Hesse-Kolloquium in Calw aus Anlass des 20. Todesjahres des Dichters, 1982*. Bad Liebenzeill [bei Calw]: B. Gegenbach

Fry, P & Long, M (1977) *Beyond the Mechanical Mind: An investigation*. Sydney, NSW: Australian Broadcasting Commission

Fukuyama, F (2012) *The End of History and the Last Man*. London: Penguin

Gaiman, N (Auth), Lewis, T. (Ed), Olson, P (Ed). (2002). *Adventures in the Dream Trade*. Framingham, Mass: NESFA Press

Gay, P (2008) *Modernism: The Lure of Heresy*. New York, NY: WW Norton

Gelpke, R (1966) *Vom Rausch im Orient und Okzident*. Stuttgart: Klett

Gelpke, R (1981) 'On travels in the universe of the soul: Reports on self-experiments with Delysid (LSD) and Psilocybin (CY)' in *Journal of Psychoactive Drugs:* 13(1): 81–89

Gelpke, R. (1966) *Vom Rausch in Orient und Okzident*. Stuttgart: Ernst Klett

Gerould, DC and Witkiewicz, SI (1992) *The Witkiewicz Reader*. Evanston, Ill: Northwestern University Press

Gray, Cecil (1924) *A Survey of Contemporary Music London*. London: Oxford University Press

Green, M (1986) *Mountain of Truth: The Counterculture Begins: Ascona 1900-1920*. London: University Press of New England

Guzmán, G (1983) *The Genus Psilocybe: A Systematic Revision of the Known Species Including the History, Distribution and Chemistry of the Hallucinogenic Species*. Vaduz: J Cramer

Harrison, JE (1890) 'Rohde's Psyche' in *The Classical Review*: Vol. 4, No. 8, 376-377

Harrison, JE (1894) 'Rohde's Psyche Part II' in *The Classical Review*: Vol. 8, No. 4, 165-166

Harrison, JE (1908). *Prolegomena to the Study of Greek Religion*. Cambridge: UK, Cambridge University Press

Harrison, JE (1912). *Themis: A Study of the Social Origins of Greek Religion*. Cambridge: UK, Cambridge University Press

Harrison, JE (1925). *Reminiscences of a Student's Life*. London: Hogarth Press

Hervier, J (1995) *The Details of Time: Conversations with Ernst Jünger*. New York, NY: Marsilio

Hervier, J (2014) *Ernst Jünger: Dans les tempêtes du siècle*. Paris: Fayard

Hesse, H (1927) *Der Steppenwolf. Roman*. Berlin: Fischer

Hesse, H, Ziolkowski, T (Editor) and Harman, M (Trans) (1992) *Soul of the Age: Selected Letters of Hermann Hesse, 1891-1962*. Farrar Straus & Giroux

Hoffman, A. (1978) Historical View on Ergot Alkaloids in *Pharmacology* (Suppl. 1): 1-11

Hofmann, A. (1979) *LSD – Mein Sorgenkind*. Stuttgart: Klett-Cotta

Hofmann, A. (1980) *LSD, My Problem Child*. New York: McGraw-Hill

Hofmann, A. (1995) Ein Dreieck Geschichte: Meine Beziehung zu Armin Mohler tagebuchblätter. In Fröschle, U. (Ed), Klein, M. J. (Ed.), Paulwitz, M. (Ed.), 1995. *Der Andere Mohler: Lesebuch fur einen Selbstdenker: Armin Mohler zum 75*. Geburtstag. Limburg a. d. Lahn: San Casciano Verlag

Hofmann, A (2009) *LSD: My Problem Child*. Santa Cruz: MAPS

Hofmann, A (2013) *LSD, My Problem Child and, Insights/Outlooks*. Oxford: Beckley Foundation / Oxford University Press

Hofmann, A. (2019) *LSD, My Problem Child and, Insights/Outlooks*. Oxford: Beckley Foundation: Oxford University Press

Hooks, B (2015) 'Eating the Other: Desire and Resistance' in *Black Looks: Race and Representation*. New York: Routledge

Horovitz, M and Joris, P (Eds) (1995) *Poems for the Millennium: The University of California book of Modern & Postmodern Poetry. Vol. 1, From Fin-de-Siècle to Negritude*. London: University of California Press

Horowitz M (1976) 'Interview with Albert Hofmann' in *High Times*: 11. Online: https://erowid.org/culture/characters/hofmann_albert/hofmann_albert_interview1.shtml

Horowitz, M, & Palmer, C (2000) *Sisters of the Extreme: Women Writing on the Drug Experience*. Rochester: Vt, Park Street Press

Huxley, A (1954) *The Doors of Perception*. New York, NY: Harper & Brothers

Huxley, A, Horowitz, M (Ed), Palmer, C (Ed) (1977) *Moksha: Aldous Huxley's Classic Writings on Psychedelics and the Visionary Experience (1931-1963)*. New York, NY: Stonehill

Isernhagen, H. (1993) 'Acid Against Established Realities: A Transcultural and Transdisciplinary View of LSD and Related Hallucinogens' in Pletscher and Ladewig (Eds), *50 Years of LSD: Current Status and Perspectives of Hallucinogens*. New York, NY: Parthenon Publishing Group

Jay, M. (2018) 'Bicycle Day Revisited'. Online: https://mikejay.net/bicycle-day-revisited/

Jay, M (2019) *Mescaline: A Global History of the First Psychedelic*. London: Yale University Press.

Jenkins, JM (2014) *The 2012 Story: The Myths, Fallacies, and Truth Behind the Most Intriguing Date in History*. New York: Jeremy P. Tarcher

Jenks, C (2003) *Transgression*. London: Routledge

Jünger, E (Auth), Moynihan, A (Trans), Söderberg, F (Illus) (2015) *Visit to Godenholm*. Stockholm: Edda Publishing

Jünger, E, Berman, RA (Editor), Friese, T (Trans) (2012) *The Adventurous Heart*. New York, NY: Telos Press

Jünger, E, Durst, D (Trans), Berman, R (Pref) (2008) *On Pain*. New York, NY: Telos Press

Jünger, E (Auth), Berman, RA (Ed), Friese, T (Trans) (2012) *The Adventurous Heart: Figures and Capriccios*. Candor, NY: Telos Press Publication

Jünger, E. Berman, RA (Editor), Friese , T (Trans) (2013) *The Forest Passage*. New York, NY: Telos Press

Karl Baier (2019) 'Early Psychonauts: Albert Hofmann's Occultic Network', Keynote lecture given at ESSWE 7 (July 2019): 7th Biennial Conference of the European Society for the Study of Western Esotericism (ESSWE), University of Amsterdam. Video is available as 'Baier Hoffmann - Early Psychonauts: Albert Hofmann's Occultic Network // ESSWE7' at https://youtu.be/1tdur8SDQ9M

Kleiner, A (2008) *The Age of Heretics: A History of The Radical Thinkers Who Reinvented Corporate Management*. San Francisco, CA: Jossey-Bass

Klüver, H (1928) *Mescal: The 'Divine' Plant and its Psychological Effects*. London: Pscheminiatures: General Series, no. 22

Klüver, H (1971) *Mescal, and Mechanisms of hallucinations*. Chicago: University of Chicago Press

König, M (Ed), Zeugin, B (Ed). (2002) *Switzerland, National Socialism and the Second World War: Final Report of the Independent Commission of Experts*. Zürich: Pendo Verlag GmbH

Kubert, J (2003) *Yossel April 19, 1943: A Story of the Warsaw Ghetto Uprising*. New York, NY: IBooks

Lattin, D (2010) *The Harvard Psychedelic Club: How Timothy Leary, Ram Dass, Huston Smith, and Andrew Weil killed the fifties and ushered in a new age for America*. New York, NY: HarperOne

Laver, J (1942) *Nostradamus or the future foretold*. London: Collins

Laver, J (1954) *The First Decadent: Being the Strange Life of J.K. Huysmans*. London: Faber & Faber

Laver, J (1963) *Museum Piece: Or the Education of an iconographer*. London: A. Deutsch

Leake, CD (1976) *What are we Living For? Practical Philosophy Vol III - The* Esthetics. NY: PJD Publications Ltd.

Leakey, FL (1992) *Baudelaire: Les Fleurs Du Mal*. New York: Cambridge University Press

Leary, T & Metzner, R (1963) 'Hermann Hesse Poet of the Interior Journey' in *The Psychedelic Review*: Vol. 1, No. 2

Leary, T (1968) *High Priest*. New York, NY: World Pub. Co.

Leary, T and Alpert, R (1963) 'The Politics of Consciousness Expansion' in *Harvard Review*: 1(4), 1963, 33–37

Leary, T. F., (1982) *Flashbacks, an autobiography*. Los Angeles, CA: JP Tarcher

Lee, MA & Shlain, B (1992) *Acid Dreams: The Complete Social History of LSD*. New York, NY: Grove Press

Leung, M (2011) *Ecstasy and Transcendence in the Postmodern State: The Search for Intimacy through Psychedelic Drugs*. Available online at: https://amanitapieces. wordpress.com/2011/07/29/ecstasy-and-transcendence-in-the-postmodern-state-the-search-for-intimacy-through-psychedelic-drugs/

Lewis, CS (1938) *Out of the Silent Planet*. London: John Lane, The Bodley Head

Lindsay, D (1976) *The Violet Apple & the Witch*. Chicago: Chicago Review Press

Lindsay, D (1987 [1922]) *The Haunted Woman*. Edinburgh: Canongate Classics

Lindsay, D (1998 [1920]) *A Voyage to Arcturus.* Edinburgh: Canongate Classics

Lindsay, D (2019 [1923]) *Sphinx*. Bookship

Loose, G (1974) *Ernst Jünger*. New York, NY: Twayne

Luhan, MD (1985) *Movers and Shakers*. Albuquerque, NM: University of New Mexico Press

Luhan, MD (1993) *Edge of Taos Desert: An Escape to Reality*. Albuquerque, NM: University of New Mexico Press

MAPS (2009) *Bulletin of the Multidisciplinary Association for Psychedelic Studies*: Vol. 9, No. 2

McKenna, TK (1992) *The Archaic Revival*. San Francisco, Calif.: HarperSanFrancisco

Milward, AS (1979) *War, Economy and Society, 1939-1945*. Berkley, CA: University of California Press

Mirrlees, H (1919). *Madeleine: One of Love's Jansenists.* London UK: W Collins Sons & Co Ltd

Mirrlees, H (1919). *Paris: A Poem*. London, UK: Hogarth Press

Mirrlees, H (1924). *The Counterplot.* London, UK: W Collins Sons & Co Ltd

Mirrlees, H (1926). *Lud-in-the-Mist.* London, UK: W Collins Sons & Co Ltd

Mirrlees, H. (Auth), Parmar, S. (Ed). (2011). *Collected Poems*. Manchester: Carcanet Press

Morat, D (2012) 'No Inner Remigration: Martin Heidegger, Ernst Jünger, and the early Federal Republic of Germany' in *Modern Intellectual History*: Vol 9, 661-69

Moriarty, DM (1993) *A Psychological Study of Adolf Hitler*. St. Louis, Mo: W.H. Green

Neaman, EA (1999) *A Dubious Past: Ernst Jünger and the politics of literature after Nazism*. Berkeley, CA: University of California Press

Newman, Paul (2009) 'The Unknown Guest'. Online: http://www.artcornwall.org/features/Paul_Newman_Unknown_Guest.htm

Nichols, D (2003) 'Hypothesis on Albert Hofmann's Famous 1943 'Bicycle Day''. Adapted from a presentation given at Mindstates IV. Online: Erowid.org/general/conferences/conference_mindstates4_nichols.shtml

Nolan, TJ (1942) 'Obituary Prof. R. Willstätter. For. Mem. R.S' in *Nature*: Vol.150

Palmer, C and Horowitz, M (2000) *Sisters of the extreme: Women Writing on the Drug Experience*. Rochester, Vt: Park Street Press

Partner, P (1982) *The Murdered Magicians: The Templars and their Myth*. Oxford: Oxford University Press

Pilkington, Mark (2009) 'Ideal Syllabus'. Online: https://www.frieze.com/article/ideal-syllabus-mark-pilkington-strange-attractor

Piper, A (2015) *Strange Drugs make for Strange Bedfellows: Ernst Jünger, Albert Hofmann and the Politics of Psychedelics*. Portland, OR: Invisible College Publishing

Piper, A (2013) 'Leo Perutz and the Mystery of St Peter's Snow' in *Time and Mind* 6(2):175-198

Prinzhorn, H (1922). *Bildnerei der Geisteskranken: Ein Beitrag zur Psychologie und Psychopathologie der Gestaltung*. Heidelberg: Springer

Prinzhorn, H (1972) *Artistry of the Mentally Ill: A Contribution to the Psychology and Psychopathology of Configuration*. Heidelberg: Springer

Rivière, P (2009) *Fulcanelli: His True Identity Revealed*. Grande Prairie, AB: Red Pill Press

Rohde, E (1925). *Psyche: the cult of souls and belief in immortality among the Greeks*. London, UK: Kegan Paul Trench, Trubner & Co Ltd

Ronson, J (2004) *The Men Who Stare at Goats*. London: Picador

Rosenfeld, AH and Foster Damon, S (1969) *William Blake: Essays for S. Foster Damon*. Providence, RI: Brown University Press

Röske, T (2004) ‚Erdentrückung 1922. Hans Prinzhorn im Meskalin-Rausch' in Jungaberle, H., Röske, T. (Hrsgg.) *Rausch im Bild - Bilderrausch: Drogen als Medien von Kunst in den 70er Jahren*. Heidelberg: Wunderhorn 117–126

Rouhier, A (1927) *La plante qui fait les yeux émerveillés: Le peyotl (Echinocactus Williamsii Lem.)*. Paris: G. Doin et cie

Sandoz (1961) *Sandoz, 1886-1961: 75 years of research and enterprise. Jubilee volume*. Sandoz Chemical Works, Inc., New York. Pharmaceutical Division

Spielberg, S (1998) *Saving Private Ryan*. Worldwide: Paramount Pictures

Schnarrenberger, C. (1987) 'Botany at the Kaiser Wilhelm Institutes‘ in Scholz, H. (1987) *Botany in Berlin*. Berlin: Botanischer Garten und Botanisches Museum Berlin-Dahlem

Sellin, B (2008) *The Life and Works of David Lindsay*. Cambridge: Cambridge University Press

Sirotkina, I (2019) *The Sixth Sense of The Avant-Garde: Dance, Kinaesthesia and The Arts in Revolutionary Russia*. New York, NY: Bloomsbury Methuen Drama

Smith, B (1994) *Peter Warlock: The Life of Philip Heseltine*. London: Clarendon Press

Smith, WA (2005) *Gossip from Across the Pond: Articles published in the United Kingdom's Gay and Lesbian Humanist, 1996–2005*. New York, N.Y: chelCpress

Spengler, O (1991) *The Decline of the West*. New York, NY: Oxford University Press

Stableford, B (2005) *Historical Dictionary of Fantasy Literature*. Lanham: Scarecrow Press

Stafford P (1983) *Psychedelics Encyclopedia*. Boston, MA: Houghton Mifflin

Stevens, J (1988) *Storming Heaven: LSD and the American Dream*. London: Heinemann

Stewart, OC (1987) *Peyote religion: A History*. Norman, OK: University of Oklahoma Press

Stoll, A (1937) *The Cardiac Glycosides*. London: Pharmaceutical Society of Great Britain

Stoll, DA (1997) *Das Hermann Hesse-Archiv von Arthur und Martha Stoll-Amsler.* Quarto 8. Hermann Hesse. Zeitschrift des Schweizerischen Literaturarchivs. Revue des Archives litteraires suisses. Bern: Schweizerisches Literaturarchiv

Straumann, L & Wildmann, Schweizer, D (2001) *Chemieunternehmen im «Dritten Reich» Swiss Chemical Enterprises in the «Third Reich»* (Publications of the ICE, volume 7). UEK / Chronos Verlag

Surette, L (1994) *The Birth of Modernism: Ezra Pound, T.S. Eliot, W.B. Yeats, and the Occult*. McGill-Queen's University Press

Swanwick, M (Auth), Gaiman, N (Pref) (2009). *Hope-In-The-Mist: The Extraordinary Career and Mysterious Life of Hope Mirrlees*, Upper Montclair, NJ: Temporary Culture

Taussig, M (2006) 'Transgression' in *Walter Benjamin's Grave*. Chicago, IL: University of Chicago Press

Thomson, V (1966) *Virgil Thomson*. New York, NY: Da Capo Press

Tommasini, A (1997) *Virgil Thomson: Composer on the Aisle*. New York, NY: W.W. Norton

Vanita, R (2007) '"Uncovenanted Joys": Catholicism, Sapphism, and Cambridge Ritualist Theory in Hope Mirrlees Madeleine One of Love's Jansenists' in Gallagher, L, Roden, F.S. & Smith, PJ *Catholic Figures, Queer Narratives*. New York: Palgrave Macmillan

Villatte, C (1895). *Parisismen: alphabetisch geordnete Sammlung der eigenartigen Ausdrucksweisen des pariser Argot.* Berlin: Langenscheidtsche Verlagsbuchhandlung

Wald, AM (1983) *The revolutionary imagination: The poetry and politics of John Wheelwright and Sherry Mangan*. Chapel Hill, NC: University of North Carolina Press

Wasson, RG, Ruck, C, Hofmann, A (1978) *The Road to Eleusis: Unveiling the Sacred Secret of the Mysteries*. New York, NY: Jovanovich

Watson, S (1993). *Strange Bedfellows: The First American Avant-Garde.* NY: Abbeville Press

Weaver, R (1977) *Spinning on a Dream Thread: Hermann Hesse, His Life and Work, and His Contact with C. G. Jung*. Perth, Western Australia: Wyvern Publications for the Analytical Psychology Club of Perth

Werthmüller, H (1950) *Der Weltprozess und die Farben: Grundriss eines Integralen Analogiesystems*. Stuttgart: Klett

Wiesen, SJ (2000) 'The Richard Willstätter Controversy: The legacy of anti-Semitism in the West German chemical industry' in J. E. Lesch (ed.) *The German Chemical Industry in the Twentieth Century*. Kluweer Academic Publishers. 347-366

Willstätter, RM, Stoll, A (Ed), Hornig, LS (Trans) (1965) *From my Life: The Memoirs of Richard Willstätter.* New York: W.A. Benjamin

Wolfe, Gary K (2007) *David Lindsay*. San Bernandino: Borgo Press

Yeide, NH (2009) *Beyond the Dreams of Avarice: the Hermann Goering collection*, Laurel Publishing

Ziolkowski, K (1974) *The Novels of Hermann Hesse: A Study in Theme and Structure*. Princeton, N.J: Princeton University Press

Ziolkowski, T (2013) *Cults and Conspiracies: A Literary History*. Baltimore: Johns Hopkins University Press

Ziolkowski, T 'Literature of Conspiracy: The Paradigm' (2013). Accessed online: https://www.berfrois.com/2013/11/theodore-ziolkowski-literature-of-conspiracy-the-paradigm/

INDEX

Printed in Great Britain
by Amazon

23117246R00081